Quick-and-Easy Christmas

To my good friend, Larry Tilley

Published in Canada by General Publishing Company, Ltd.,
30 Lesmill Road, Don Mills, Toronto, Ontario.
Published in the United Kingdom by Constable and Company, Ltd.

Quick-and-Easy Christmas Charted Designs is a new
work, first published by Dover Publications, Inc., in 1990.

Manufactured in the United States of America
Dover Publications, Inc.
31 East 2nd Street
Mineola, N.Y. 11501

Library of Congress Cataloging-in-Publication Data

Christopher, Barbara.
Quick-and-easy Christmas charted designs / by Barbara Christopher.
p. cm. — (Dover needlework series)
ISBN 0-486-26419-X
1. Embroidery—Patterns. 2. Christmas in art. I. Title. II. Series.
TT773.C5386 1990 90-3130
746.44—dc20 CIP

Introduction

Christmas is one of the most festive seasons of the year. Traditionally, handmade gifts and one-of-a-kind decorations have played an important role in the celebrations. In today's busy world, few of us have the time we would like for elaborate preparations for the holidays. With this new collection of charted designs from Barbara Christopher, however, you can stitch a Christmas heirloom in a fraction of the time you would expect it to take.

Santa, stockings, wreaths, trees, bells, holly—all these well-loved Christmas motifs, plus many more, are presented here as simple, yet effective, easy-to-make charted designs. Use them to decorate ornaments, Christmas cards, placemats, tree skirts, pillows and other holiday items.

Most of these designs were originally created for counted cross-stitch, but they are easily translated into other needlework techniques. Keep in mind that the finished piece will not be the same size as the charted design unless you are working on fabric or canvas with the same number of threads per inch as the chart has squares per inch. With knitting and crocheting, the size will vary according to the number of stitches per inch.

COUNTED CROSS-STITCH

MATERIALS

1. **Needles.** A small blunt tapestry needle, No. 24 or No. 26.

2. **Fabric.** Evenweave linen, cotton, wool or synthetic fabrics all work well. The most popular fabrics are aida cloth, linen and hardanger cloth. Cotton aida is most commonly available in 18 threads-per-inch, 14 threads-per-inch and 11 threads-per-inch (14-count is the most popular size). Evenweave linen comes in a variety of threads-per-inch. To work cross-stitch on linen involves a slightly different technique (see page 4). Thirty thread-per-inch linen will result in a stitch about the same size as 14-count aida. Hardanger cloth has 22 threads to the inch and is available in cotton or linen. The amount of fabric needed depends on the size of the cross-stitch design. To determine yardage, divide the number of stitches in the design by the thread-count of the fabric. For example: If a design 112 squares wide by 140 squares deep is worked on a 14-count fabric, divide 112 by 14 (= 8), and 140 by 14 (= 10). The design will measure 8″ × 10″. The same design worked on 22-count fabric measures about 5″ × 6½″. When cutting the fabric, be sure to allow at least 2″ of blank fabric all around the design for finishing.

3. **Threads and Yarns.** Six-strand embroidery floss, crewel wool, Danish Flower Thread, pearl cotton or metallic threads all work well for cross-stitch. DMC Embroidery Floss has been used to color-code the patterns in this volume. Crewel wool works well on evenweave wool fabric. Danish Flower Thread is a thicker thread with a matte finish, one strand equaling two of embroidery floss. In some designs, Balger Metallic Yarn* can be used to add sparkle.

4. **Embroidery Hoop.** A wooden or plastic 4″, 5″ or 6″ round or oval hoop with a screw-type tension adjuster works best for cross-stitch.

5. **Scissors.** A pair of sharp embroidery scissors is essential to all embroidery.

PREPARING TO WORK

To prevent raveling, either whip stitch or machine-stitch the outer edges of the fabric.

Locate the exact center of the chart (many of the charts in this book have an arrow at the top or bottom and side; follow these arrows to their intersection to locate the chart center). Establish the center of the fabric by folding it in half first vertically, then horizontally. The center stitch of the chart falls where the creases of the fabric meet. Mark the fabric center with a basting thread.

It is best to begin cross-stitch at the top of the design. To establish the top, count the squares up from the center of the chart, and the corresponding number of holes up from the center of the fabric.

Place the fabric tautly in the embroidery hoop, for tension makes it easier to push the needle through the holes without piercing the fibers. While working continue to retighten the fabric as necessary.

When working with multiple strands (such as embroidery floss) always separate (strand) the thread before beginning to stitch. This one small step allows for better coverage of the fabric. When you need more than one thread in the needle, use separate strands and do not double the thread. (For example: If you need four strands, use four separated strands.) Thread has a nap (just as fabrics do) and can be felt to be smoother in one direction than the other. Always work with the nap (the smooth side) pointing down.

For 14-count aida and 30-count linen, work with two strands of six-strand floss. For more texture, use more thread; for a flatter look, use less thread.

---

*For information on where to obtain Balger Metallic Yarn write to Kreinik Manufacturing Co., Inc., Dept. D2, P.O. Box 1966, Parkersburg, West Virginia 26102.

EMBROIDERY

To begin, fasten the thread with a waste knot and hold a short length of thread on the underside of the work, anchoring it with the first few stitches (*Diagram 1*). When the thread end is securely in place, clip the knot.

DIAGRAM 1
Reverse side of work

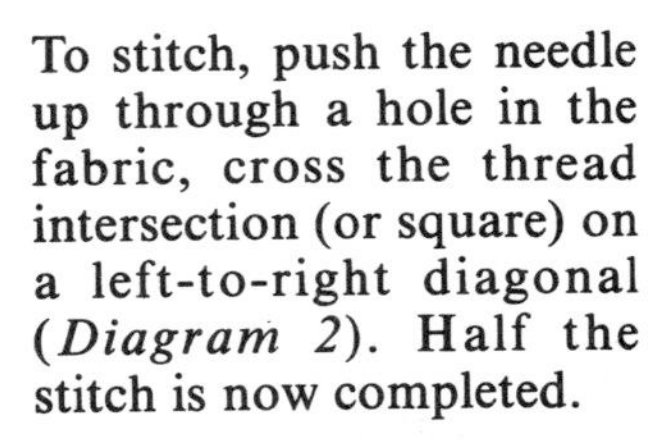

To stitch, push the needle up through a hole in the fabric, cross the thread intersection (or square) on a left-to-right diagonal (*Diagram 2*). Half the stitch is now completed.

DIAGRAM 2

Next, cross back, right to left, forming an X (*Diagram 3*).

Work all the same color stitches on one row, then cross back, completing the X's (*Diagram 4*).

DIAGRAM 3

DIAGRAM 4

Some needleworkers prefer to cross each stitch as they come to it. This method also works, but be sure all of the top stitches are slanted in the same direction. Isolated stitches must be crossed as they are worked. Vertical stitches are crossed as shown in *Diagram 5*.

DIAGRAM 5

At the top, work horizontal rows of a single color, left to right. This method allows you to go from an unoccupied space to an occupied space (working from an empty hole to a filled one), making ruffling of the floss less likely. Holes are used more than once, and all stitches "hold hands" unless a space is indicated on the chart. Hold the work upright throughout (do not turn as with many needlepoint stitches).

When carrying the thread from one area to another, run the needle under a few stitches on the wrong side. Do not carry thread across an open expanse of fabric as it will be visible from the front when the project is completed.

To end a color, weave in and out of the underside of the stitches, making a scallop stitch or two for extra security (*Diagram 6*). When possible, end in the same direction in which you were working, jumping up a row if necessary (*Diagram 7*). This prevents holes caused by stitches being pulled in two directions. Trim the thread ends closely and do not leave any tails or knots as they will show through the fabric when the work is completed.

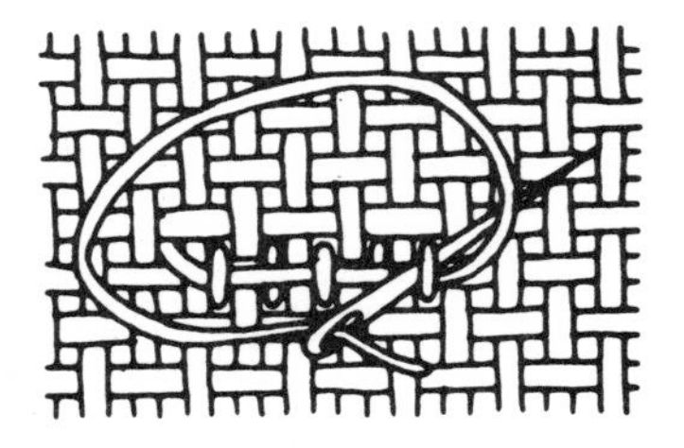

DIAGRAM 6
Reverse side of work

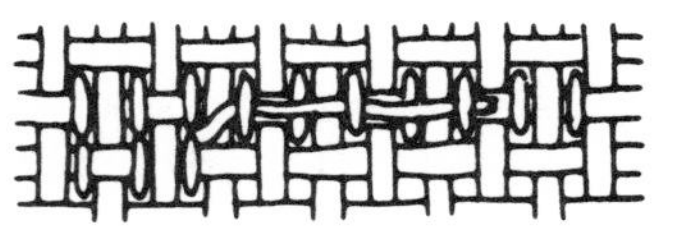

DIAGRAM 7
Reverse side of work

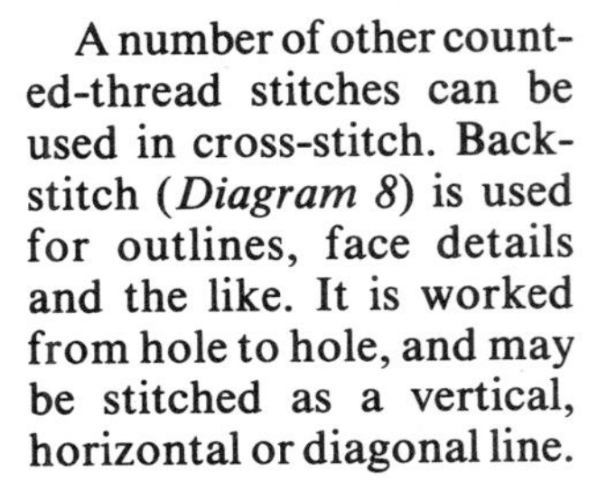

A number of other counted-thread stitches can be used in cross-stitch. Backstitch (*Diagram 8*) is used for outlines, face details and the like. It is worked from hole to hole, and may be stitched as a vertical, horizontal or diagonal line.

DIAGRAM 8

Straight stitch is worked from side to side over several threads (*Diagram 9*) and affords solid coverage.

DIAGRAM 9

French knots (*Diagram 10*) are handy for special effects. They are worked in the same manner as on regular embroidery.

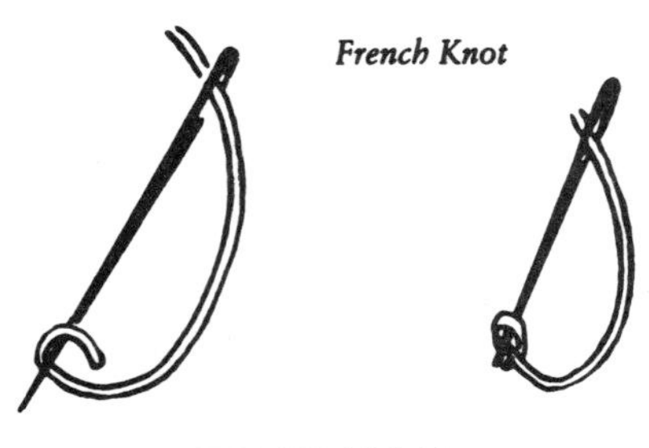

DIAGRAM 10

Embroidery on Linen. Working on linen requires a slightly different technique. While evenweave linen is remarkably regular, there are always a few thick or thin threads. To keep the stitches even, cross-stitch is worked over two threads in each direction (*Diagram 11*).

DIAGRAM 11

As you are working over more threads, linen affords a greater variation in stitches. A half-stitch can slant in either direction and is uncrossed. A three-quarters stitch is shown in *Diagram 12*.

DIAGRAM 12

Diagram 13 shows the backstitch worked on linen.

DIAGRAM 13

Embroidery on Gingham. Gingham and other checked fabrics can be used for cross-stitch. Using the fabric as a guide, work the stitches from corner to corner of each check.

Embroidery on Uneven-Weave Fabrics. If you wish to work cross-stitch on an uneven-weave fabric, baste a lightweight Penelope needlepoint canvas to the material. The design can then be stitched by working the cross-stitch over the double mesh of the canvas. When working in this manner, take care not to catch the threads of the canvas in the embroidery. After the cross-stitch is completed, remove the basting threads. With tweezers remove first the vertical threads, one strand at a time, of the needlepoint canvas, then the horizontal threads.

NEEDLEPOINT

One of the most common methods for working needlepoint is from a charted design. By simply viewing each square of a chart as a stitch on the canvas, the patterns quickly and easily translate from one technique to another.

MATERIALS

1. **Needles.** A blunt tapestry needle with a rounded tip and an elongated eye. The needle must clear the hole of the canvas without spreading the threads. For No. 10 canvas, a No. 18 needle works best.
2. **Canvas.** There are two distinct types of needlepoint canvas: single-mesh (mono canvas) and double-mesh (Penelope canvas). Single-mesh canvas, the more common of the two, is easier on the eyes as the spaces are slightly larger. Double-mesh canvas has two horizontal and two vertical threads forming each mesh. The latter is a very stable canvas on which the threads stay securely in place as the work progresses. Canvas is available in many sizes, from 5 mesh-per-inch to 18 mesh-per-inch, and even smaller. The number of mesh-per-inch will, of course, determine the dimensions of the finished needlepoint project. A 60 square × 120 square chart will measure 12″ × 24″ on 5 mesh-to-the-inch canvas, 5″ × 10″ on 12 mesh-to-the-inch canvas. The most common canvas size is 10 to the inch.
3. **Yarns.** Persian, crewel and tapestry yarns all work well on needlepoint canvas.

PREPARING TO WORK

Allow 1″ to 1½″ blank canvas all around. Bind the raw edges of the canvas with masking tape or machine-stitched double-fold bias tape.

There are few hard-and-fast rules on where to begin the design. It is best to complete the main motif, then fill in the background as the last step.

For any guidelines you wish to draw on the canvas, take care that your marking medium is waterproof. Non-soluble inks, acrylic paints thinned with water so as not to clog the mesh, and waterproof felt-tip pens all work well. If unsure, experiment on a scrap of canvas.

When working with multiple strands (such as Persian yarn) always separate (strand) the yarn before beginning to stitch. This one small step allows for better coverage of the canvas. When you need more than one piece of yarn in the needle, use separate strands and do not double the yarn. For example: If you need two strands of 3-ply Persian yarn, use two separated strands. Yarn has a nap (just as fabrics do) and can be felt to be smoother in one direction than the other. Always work with the nap (the smooth side) pointing down.

For 5 mesh-to-the-inch canvas, use six strands of 3-ply yarn; for 10 mesh-to-the-inch canvas, use three strands of 3-ply yarn.

STITCHING

Cut yarn lengths 18″ long. Begin needlepoint by holding about 1″ of loose yarn on the wrong side of the work and working the first several stitches over the loose end to secure it. To end a piece of yarn, run it under several completed stitches on the wrong side of the work.

There are hundreds of needlepoint stitch variations, but tent stitch is universally considered to be *the* needlepoint stitch. The most familiar versions of tent stitch are half-cross stitch, continental stitch and basket-weave stitch.

Half-cross stitch (*Diagram 14*) is worked from left to right. The canvas is then turned around and the return row is again stitched from left to right. Holding the needle vertically, bring it to the front of the canvas through the hole that will be the bottom of the first stitch. Keep the stitches loose for minimum distortion and good coverage. Half-cross stitch is best worked on a double-mesh canvas.

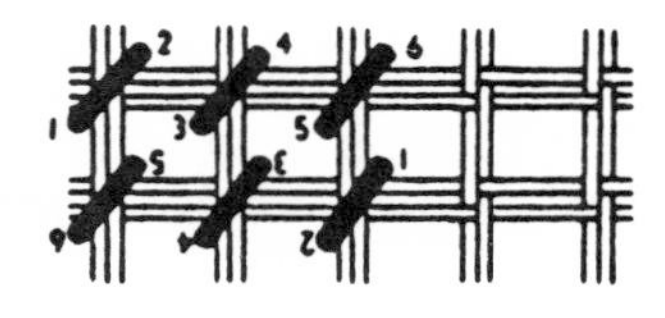

DIAGRAM 14

Continental stitch (*Diagram 15*) begins in the upper right-hand corner and is worked from right to left. The needle is slanted and always brought out a mesh ahead. The resulting stitch appears as a half-cross stitch on the front and as a slanting stitch on the back. When the row is complete, turn the canvas around to work the return row, continuing to stitch from right to left.

DIAGRAM 15

Basket-weave stitch (*Diagram 16*) begins in the upper right-hand corner with four continental stitches (two stitches worked horizontally across the top and two placed directly below the first stitch). Work diagonal rows, the first slanting up and across the canvas from right to left, and the next down and across from left to right. Moving down the canvas from left to right, the needle is in a vertical position; working in the opposite direction, the needle is horizontal. The rows interlock, creating a basket-weave pattern on the wrong side. If the stitch is not done properly, a faint ridge will show where the pattern was interrupted. On basket-weave stitch, always stop working in the middle of a row, rather than at the end, so that you will know in which direction you were working.

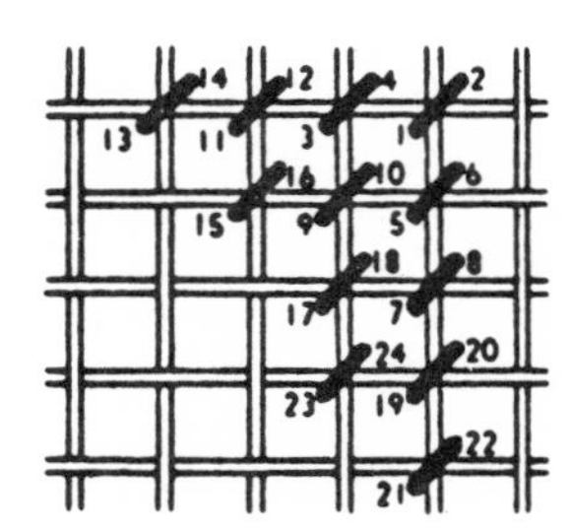

DIAGRAM 16

KNITTING

Charted designs can be worked into stockinette stitch as you are knitting, or they can be embroidered with duplicate stitch when the knitting is complete. For the former, wind the different colors of yarn on bobbins and work in the same manner as in Fair Isle knitting. A few quick Fair Isle tips: (1) Always bring up the new color yarn from under the dropped color to prevent holes. (2) Carry the color not in use loosely across the wrong side of the work, but not more than three or four stitches without twisting the yarns. If a color is not in use for more than seven or eight stitches, it is usually best to drop that color yarn and rejoin a new bobbin when the color is again needed.

CROCHET

There are a number of ways in which charts can be used for crochet. Among them are:

SINGLE CROCHET

Single crochet is often seen worked in multiple colors. When changing colors, always pick up the new color for the last yarn-over of the old color. The color not in use can be carried loosely across the back of the work for a few stitches, or you can work the single crochet over the unused color. The latter method makes for a neater appearance on the wrong side, but sometimes the old color peeks through the stitches. This method can also be applied to half-double crochet and double crochet, but keep in mind that the longer stitches will distort the design.

FILET CROCHET

This technique is nearly always worked from charts and uses only one color thread. The result is a solid-color piece with the design filled in and the background left as an open mesh. Care must be taken in selecting the design, as the longer stitch causes distortion.

AFGHAN CROCHET

The most common method here is cross-stitch worked over the afghan stitch. Complete the afghan crochet project. Then, following the chart for color placement, work cross-stitch over the squares of crochet.

OTHER CHARTED METHODS

Latch hook, Assisi embroidery, beading, cross-stitch on needlepoint canvas (a European favorite) and lace net embroidery are among the other needlework methods worked from charts.

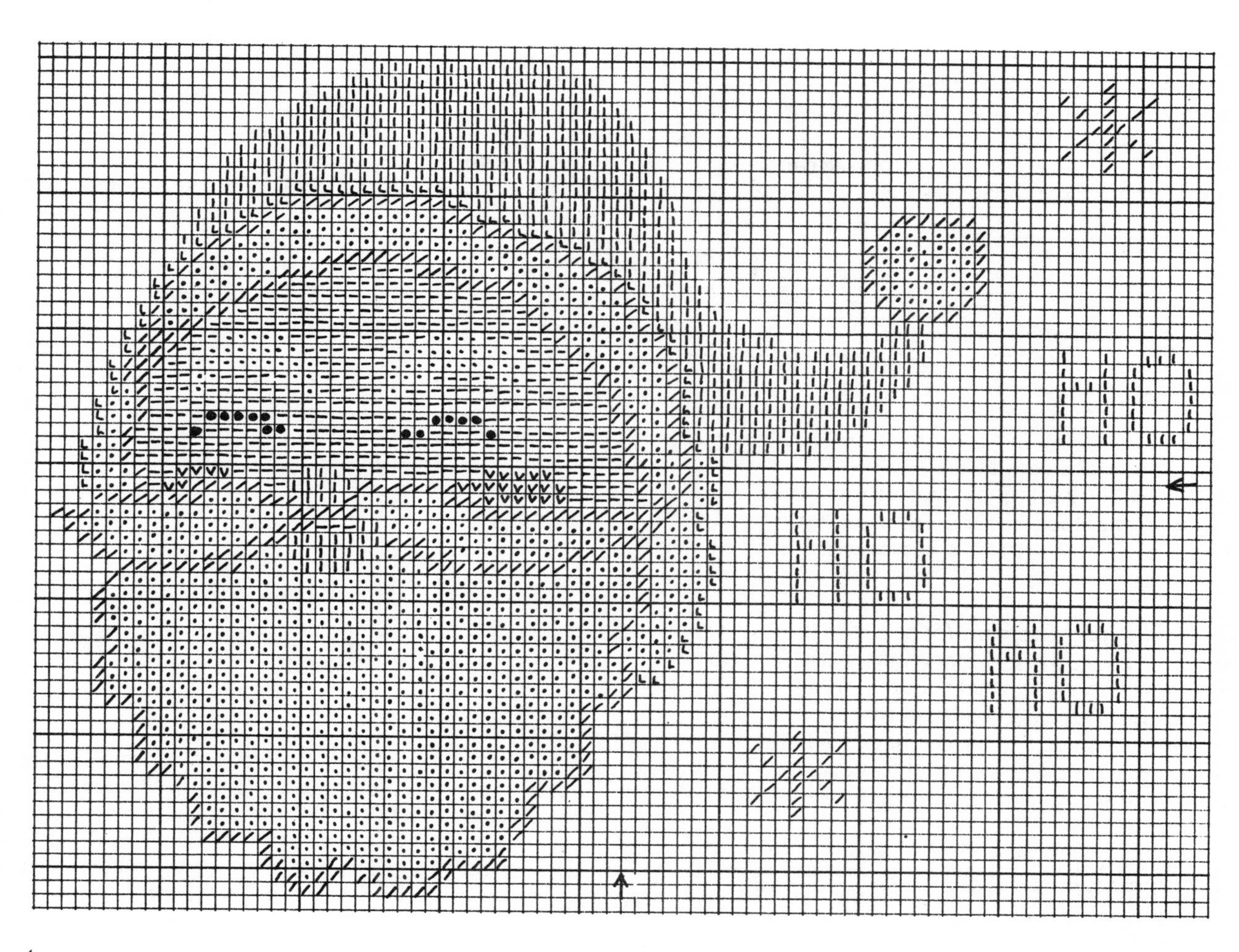

Santa ▲

82 stitches by 62 stitches

	DMC #	
V	352	Light Coral
–	353	Peach
I	666	Bright Christmas Red
/	775	Light Baby Blue
●	825	Dark Blue
L	3325	Baby Blue
•		White

Lantern and Poinsettia ▸

29 stitches by 45 stitches

	DMC #	
●	310	Black
S	666	Bright Christmas Red
I	740	Tangerine
O	743	Dark Yellow
X	816	Garnet Red
◣	910	Dark Emerald Green
/	913	Medium Nile Green
L	995	Dark Electric Blue

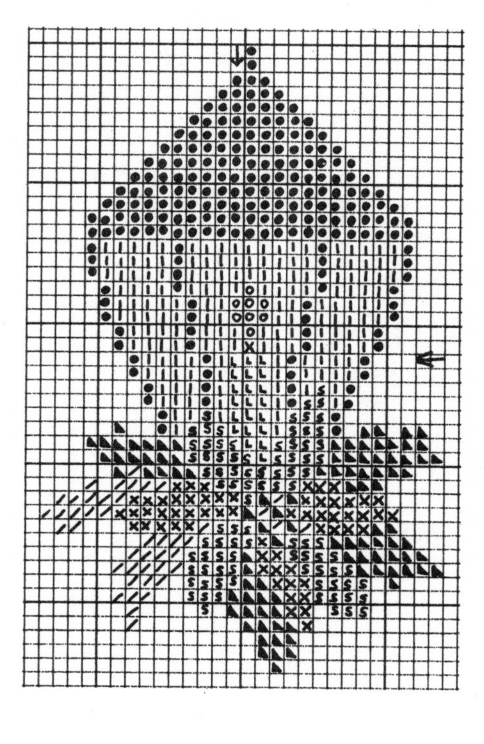

Toy Soldier Border ▲

23-stitch repeat by 47 stitches

BACK-STITCH	CROSS-STITCH	DMC #	
~~	●	310	Black
	✚	517	Medium Wedgwood Blue
	ϵ	518	Light Wedgwood Blue
	N	606	Bright Orange Red
. . .	I	608	Bright Orange
	—	754	Light Peach
	◐	780	Very Dark Topaz
——	V	783	Christmas Gold
	◣	909	Very Dark Emerald Green
	S	911	Medium Emerald Green
–|–|–	/	913	Medium Nile Green
	·		White

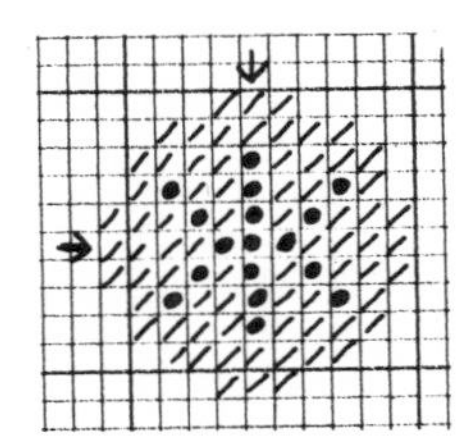

▲ Snowflake in a Circle

11 stitches by 11 stitches

	DMC #	
●	995	Dark Electric Blue
/	996	Medium Electric Blue

▼ Reindeer

43 stitches by 50 stitches

BACK-STITCH	CROSS-STITCH	DMC #	
– – – –	◣	310	Black
	M	351	Coral
	S	434	Light Brown
	I	436	Tan
~~	L	606	Bright Orange Red
	✳	611	Dark Drab Brown
	/	612	Medium Drab Brown
	N	701	Light Christmas Green
	K	801	Dark Coffee Brown
	●	995	Dark Electric Blue

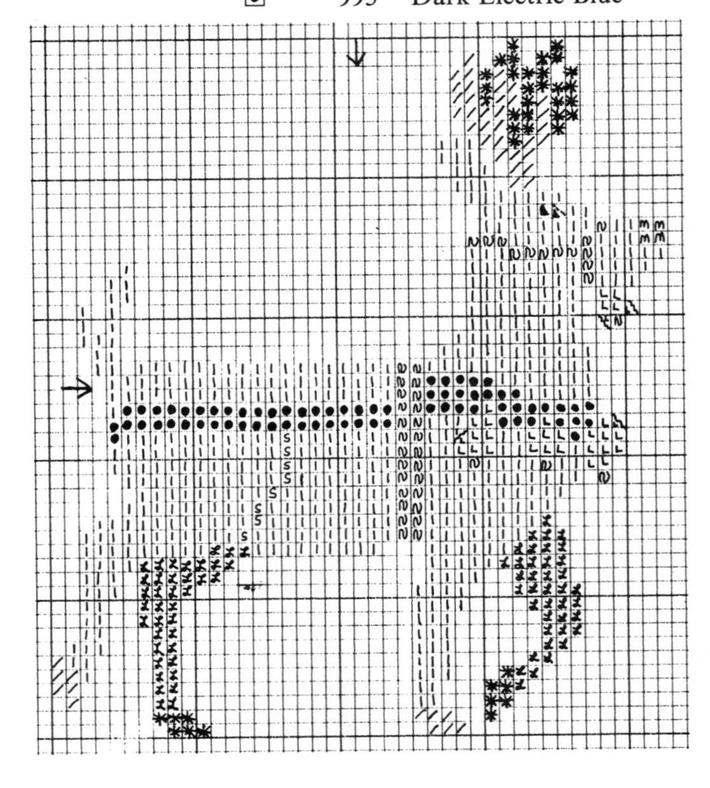

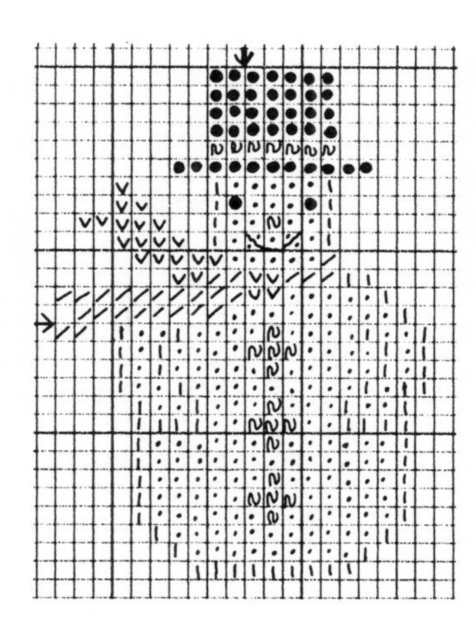

◂ *Snowman*

20 stitches by 28 stitches

BACK-STITCH	CROSS-STITCH	DMC #	
∿∿∿	∾	606	Bright Orange Red
	●	796	Dark Royal Blue
	|	800	Pale Delft Blue
	V	910	Dark Emerald Green
	/	912	Light Emerald Green
	·		White

▾ *Santa's Sleigh*

78 stitches by 51 stitches

FRENCH KNOT	CROSS-STITCH	DMC #	
	P	581	Moss Green
•	|	606	Bright Orange Red
	L	666	Bright Christmas Red
	◤	700	Bright Christmas Green
	∾	704	Bright Chartreuse
	S	725	Topaz
	V	740	Tangerine
	⋌	743	Dark Yellow
	–	754	Light Peach
	◣	816	Garnet Red
	/	912	Light Emerald Green
□	●	995	Dark Electric Blue
	♡	996	Medium Electric Blue
	·		White

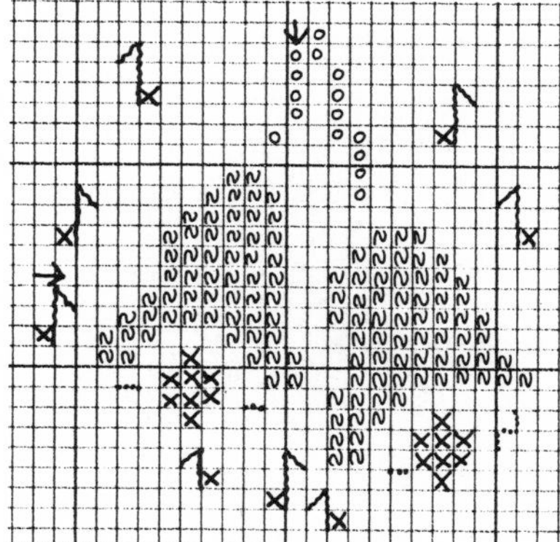

Bells ▴

25 stitches by 25 stitches

BACK-STITCH	CROSS-STITCH	DMC #	
· · ·	∾	606	Bright Orange Red
	o	742	Light Tangerine
∿∿∿	X	911	Medium Emerald Green

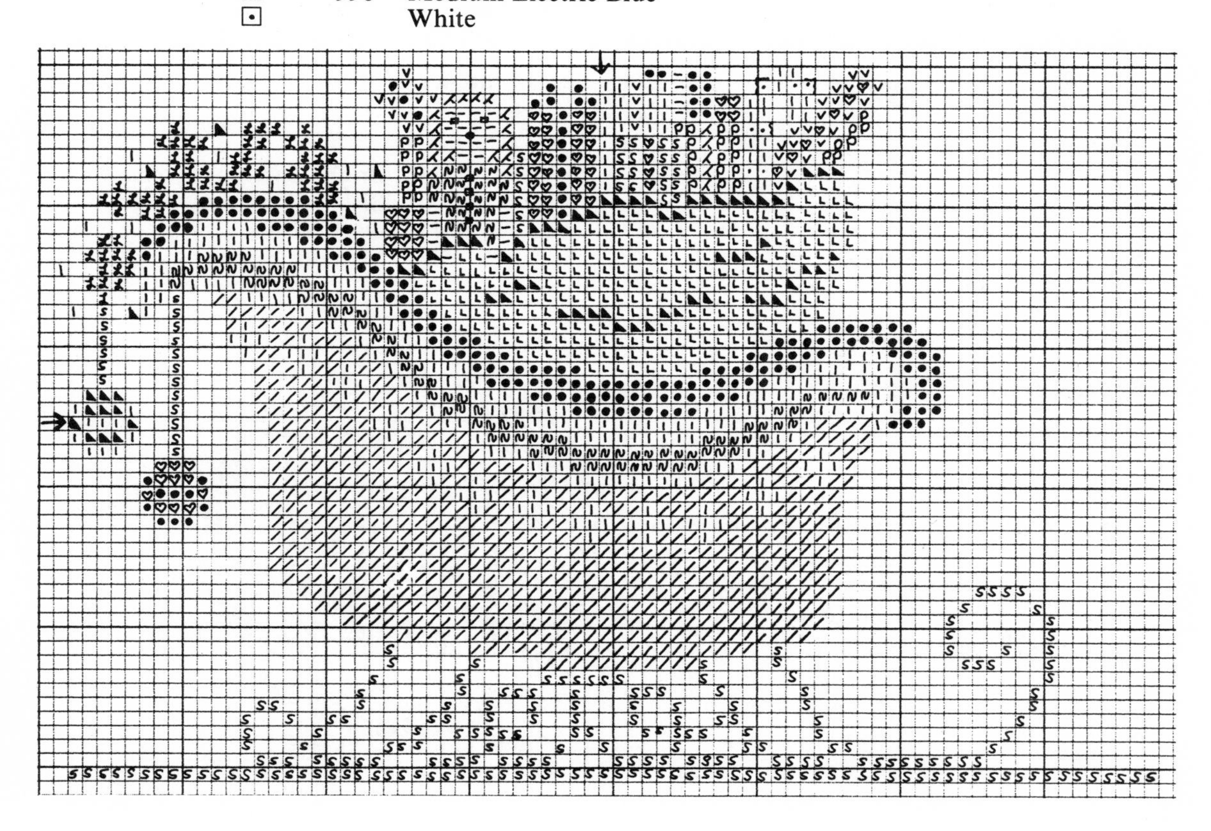

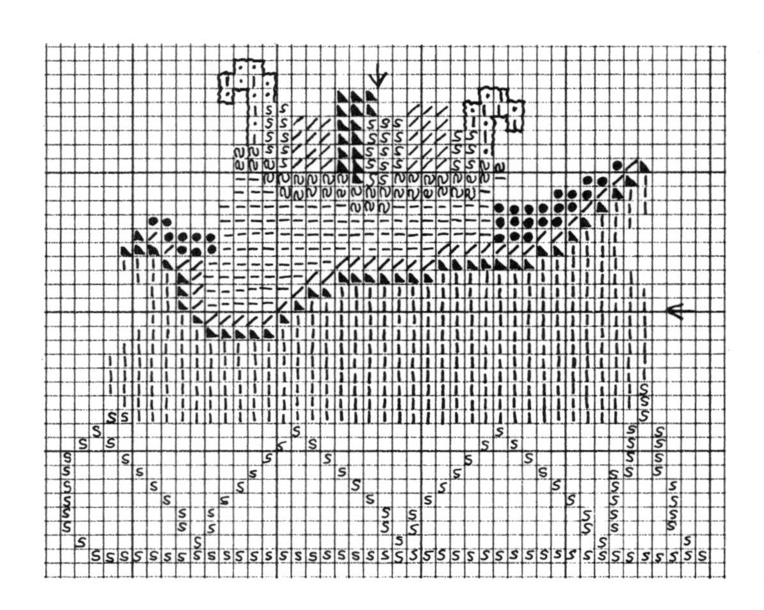

Sleigh

46 stitches by 36 stitches

BACK-STITCH	CROSS-STITCH	DMC #	
	■ (dot)	311	Medium Navy Blue
~~	▯ (I)	606	Bright Orange Red
	N	666	Bright Christmas Red
	S	783	Christmas Gold
	◣	815	Medium Garnet Red
	—	911	Medium Emerald Green
	/	913	Medium Nile Green
	·		White

Snow Scene

37 stitches by 27 stitches

BACK-STITCH	CROSS-STITCH	DMC #	
•—•—•	N	300	Very Dark Mahogany
	o	444	Dark Lemon Yellow
	·	827	Very Light Blue
——	X	911	Medium Emerald Green
~~	●	975	Dark Golden Brown
	I	976	Medium Golden Brown
	—	977	Light Golden Brown
	/		White

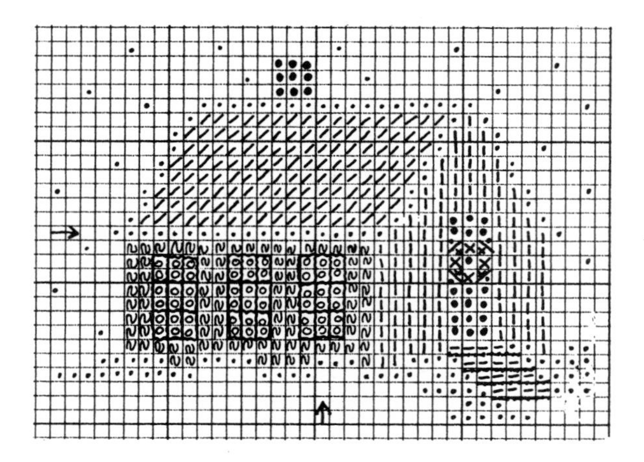

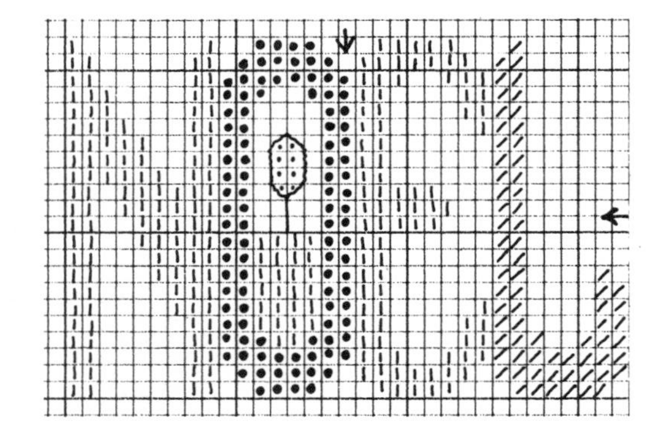

Noel

33 stitches by 22 stitches

BACK-STITCH	CROSS-STITCH	DMC #	
	I	666	Bright Christmas Red
——	●	700	Bright Christmas Green
~~	·	743	Dark Yellow
	/	826	Medium Blue

Merry Noel Wreath

28 stitches by 28 stitches

BACK-STITCH	CROSS-STITCH	DMC #	
~~	—	666	Bright Christmas Red
	●	699	Christmas Green
	V	702	Kelly Green
	/	704	Bright Chartreuse
	o	725*	Topaz
	I	740	Tangerine

*If desired, replace 725 Topaz with Balger #8 braid, Gold #002.

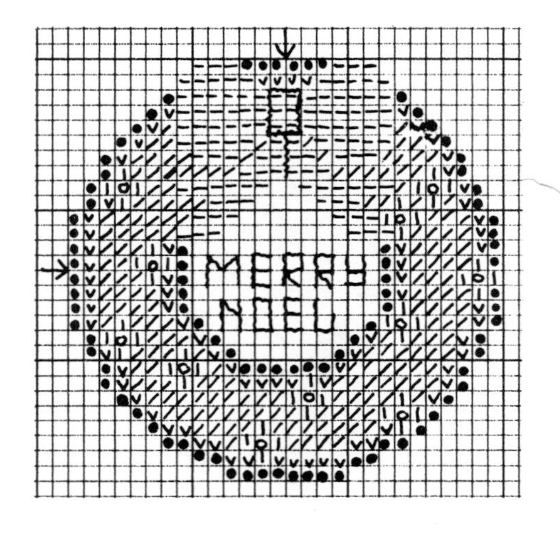

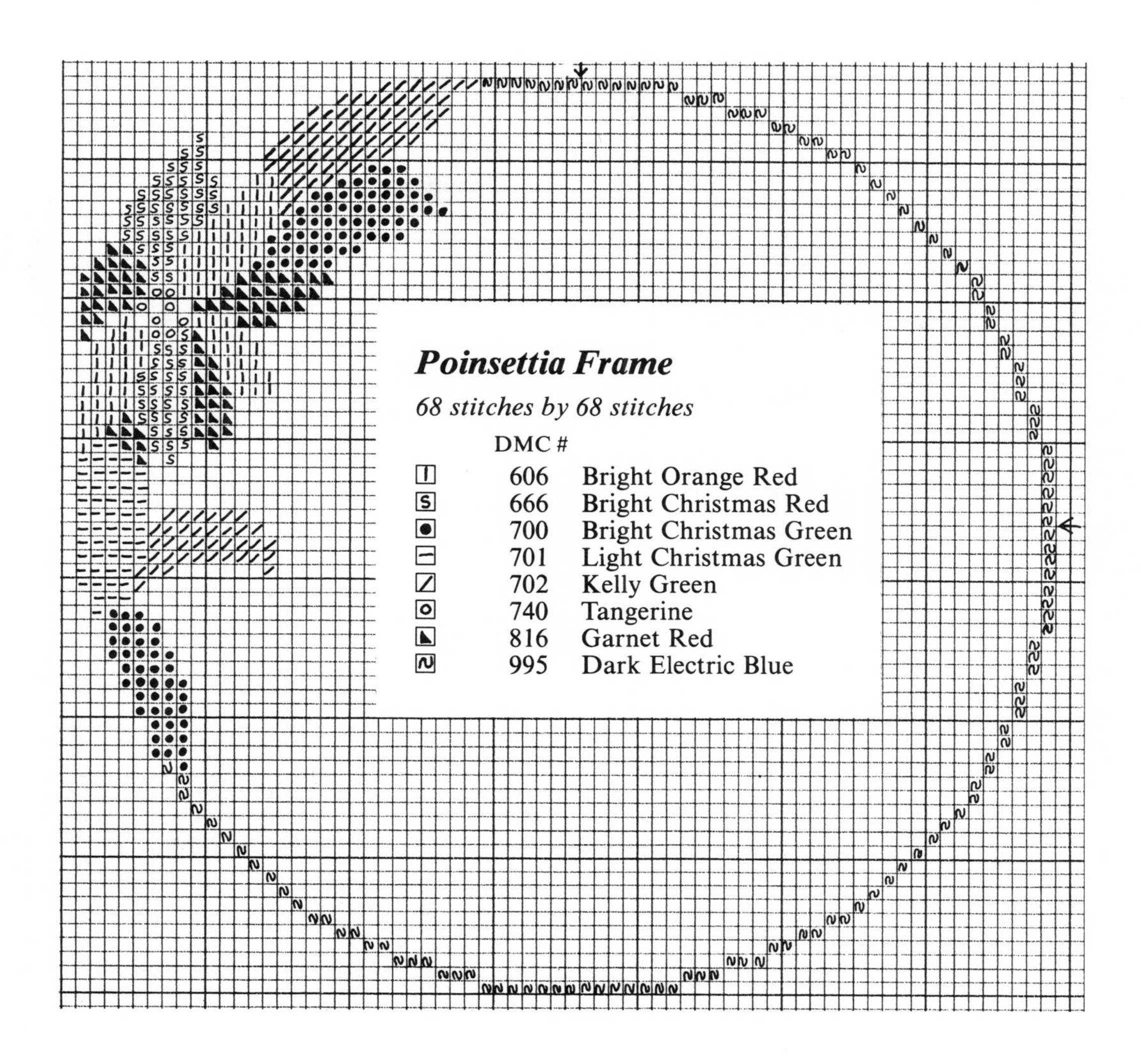

Poinsettia Frame

68 stitches by 68 stitches

DMC #	
606	Bright Orange Red
666	Bright Christmas Red
700	Bright Christmas Green
701	Light Christmas Green
702	Kelly Green
740	Tangerine
816	Garnet Red
995	Dark Electric Blue

Stocking ▼

17 stitches by 28 stitches

DMC #	
444	Dark Lemon Yellow
666	Bright Christmas Red
700	Bright Christmas Green
702	Kelly Green
827	Very Light Blue
996	Medium Electric Blue

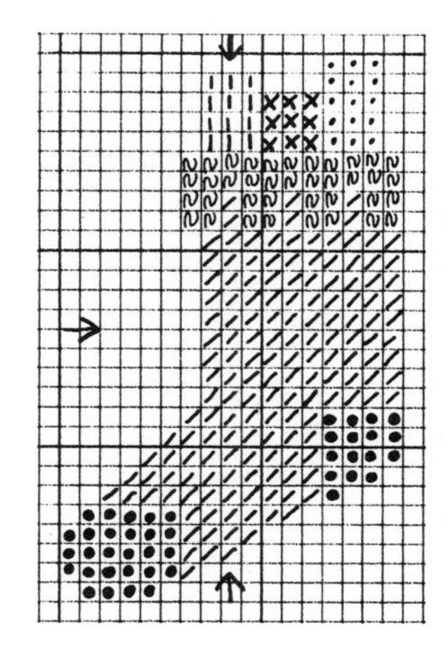

Toy Soldier ▶

12 stitches by 30 stitches

FRENCH KNOT	BACK-STITCH	CROSS-STITCH	DMC #	
			304	Medium Christmas Red
•	—		310	Black
			353	Peach
			413	Dark Pewter Gray
	∿∿∿		606	Bright Orange Red
			725	Topaz
			781	Dark Topaz
			905	Dark Parrot Green
			906	Medium Parrot Green
				White

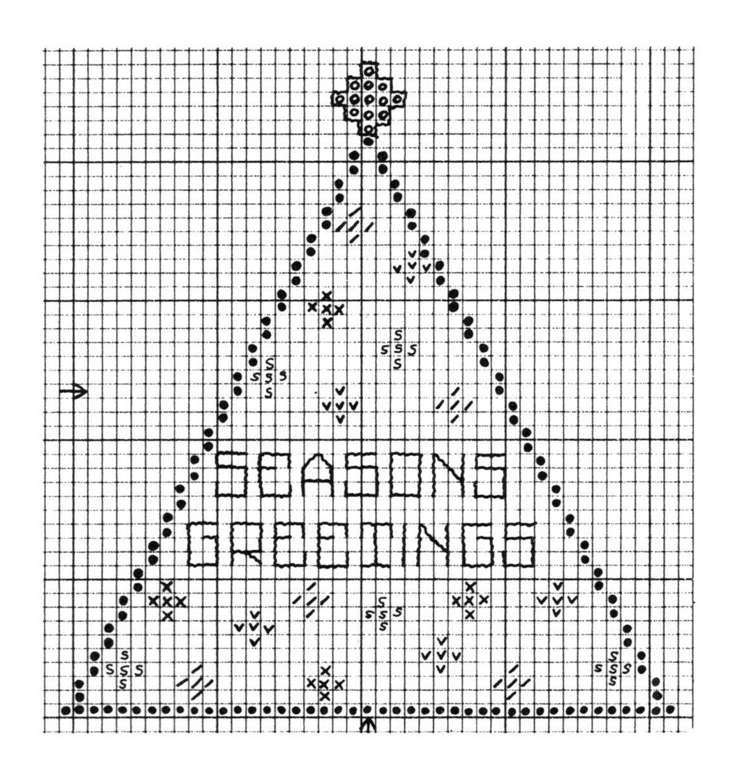

◂ *Season's Greetings*

43 stitches by 47 stitches

BACK-STITCH	CROSS-STITCH	DMC #	
	S	209	Dark Lavender
	o	444	Dark Lemon Yellow
	V	666	Bright Christmas Red
	/	740	Tangerine
	X	826	Medium Blue
∿∿∿	●	910	Dark Emerald Green

Silent Night ▸

36 stitches by 35 stitches

BACK-STITCH	CROSS-STITCH	DMC #	
	S	434	Light Brown
	/	437	Light Tan
∿∿∿	Δ	444*	Dark Lemon Yellow
	N	666	Bright Christmas Red
	o	741	Medium Tangerine
	●	825	Dark Blue
	I	828	Very Pale Blue
	·		White

*If desired, replace 444 Dark Lemon Yellow with Balger braid #8, Gold #002.

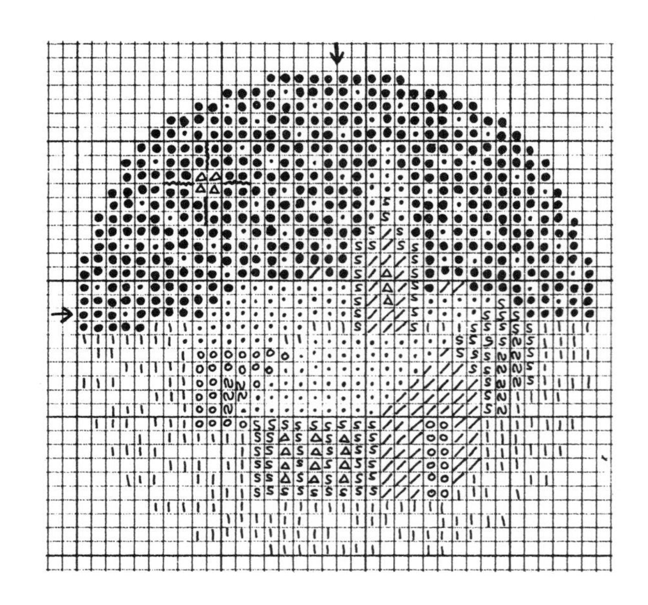

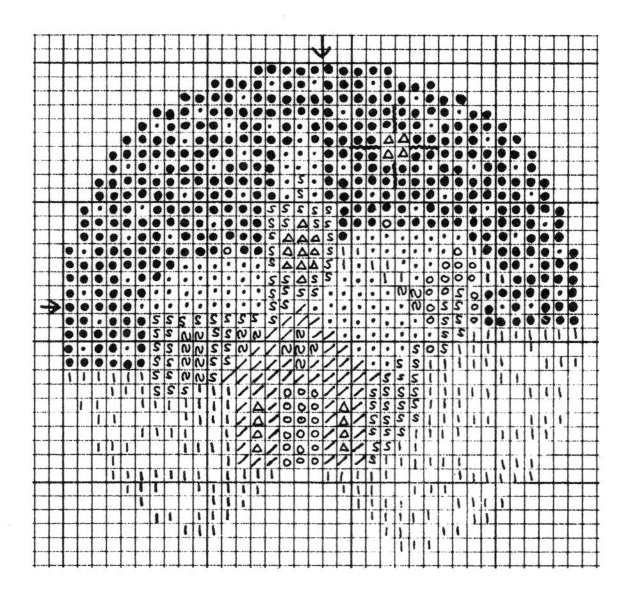

◂ *All Is Calm*

36 stitches by 35 stitches

BACK-STITCH	CROSS-STITCH	DMC #	
	S	434	Light Brown
	/	437	Light Tan
∿∿∿	Δ	444*	Dark Lemon Yellow
	N	666	Bright Christmas Red
	o	741	Medium Tangerine
	●	825	Dark Blue
	I	828	Very Pale Blue
	·		White

*If desired, replace 444 Dark Lemon Yellow with Balger braid #8, Gold #002.

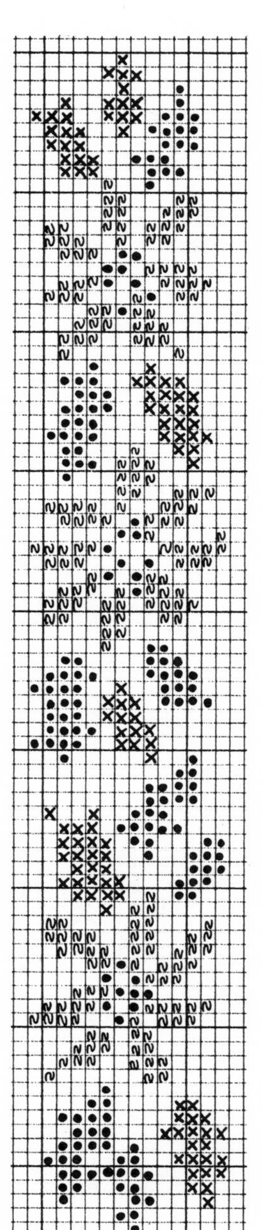

Holly and Poinsettia Border

14 stitches by 85 stitches

	DMC #	
∾	666	Bright Christmas Red
●	909	Very Dark Emerald Green
☒	911	Medium Emerald Green

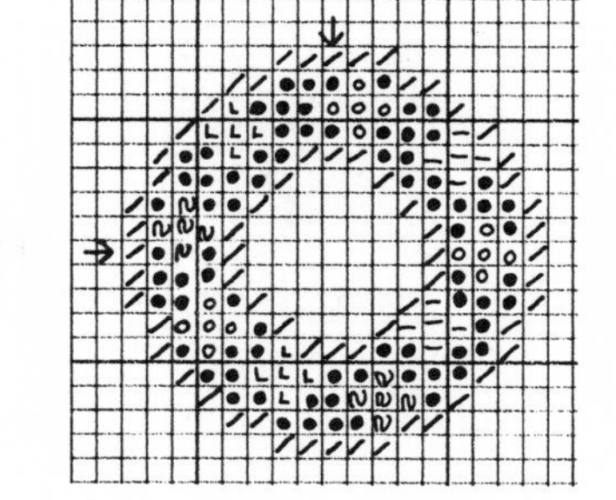

Small Wreath

17 stitches by 17 stitches

	DMC #	
S	606	Bright Orange Red
●	700	Bright Christmas Green
⁄	704	Bright Chartreuse
L	740	Tangerine
o	742	Light Tangerine
–	827	Very Light Blue

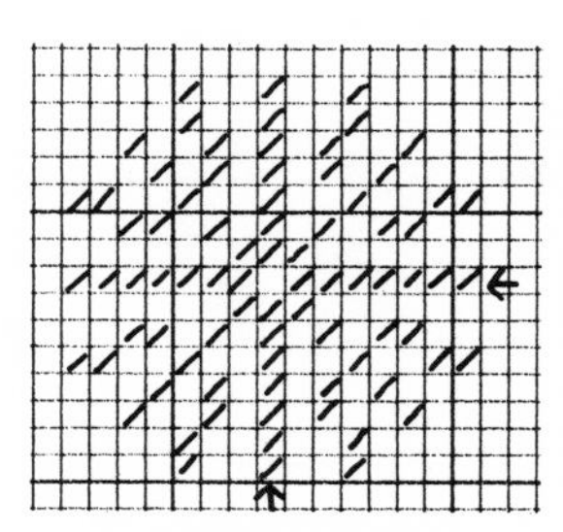

Snowflake

15 stitches by 15 stitches

	DMC #	
⁄	827	Very Light Blue

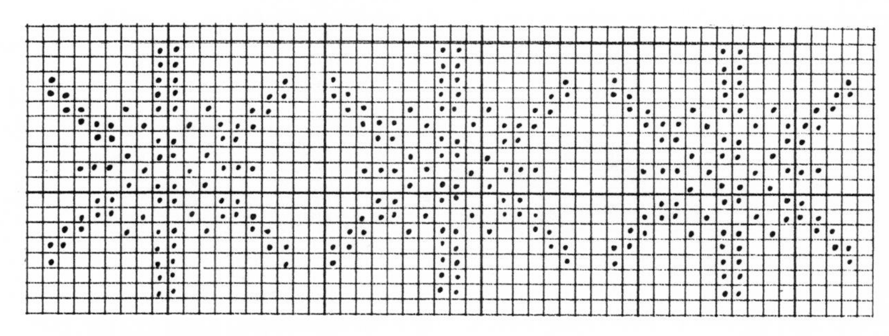

Snowflake Border

18-stitch repeat by 17 stitches

	DMC #	
·	828	Very Pale Blue

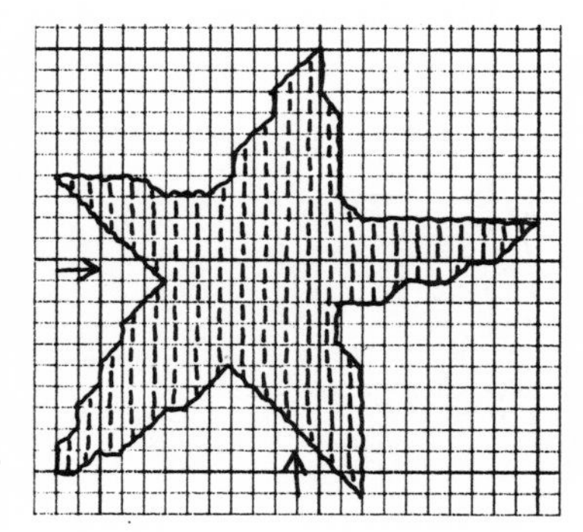

Star

22 stitches by 20 stitches

BACK-STITCH	CROSS-STITCH	DMC #	
∿∿∿	I	606	Bright Orange Red

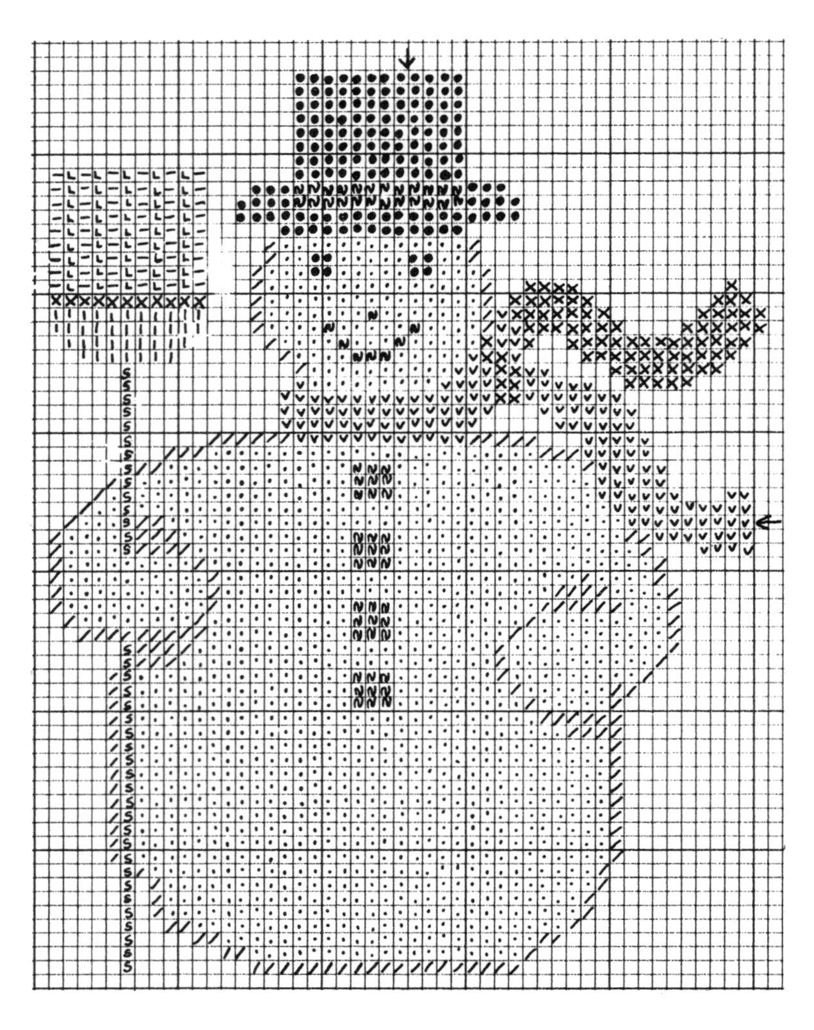

◂ ***Snowman***

50 stitches by 65 stitches

	DMC #	
●	310	Black
S	400	Dark Mahogany
L	647	Medium Beaver Gray
N	666	Bright Christmas Red
X	702	Kelly Green
V	704	Bright Chartreuse
I	783	Christmas Gold
—	822	Light Beige Gray
/	828	Very Pale Blue
·		White

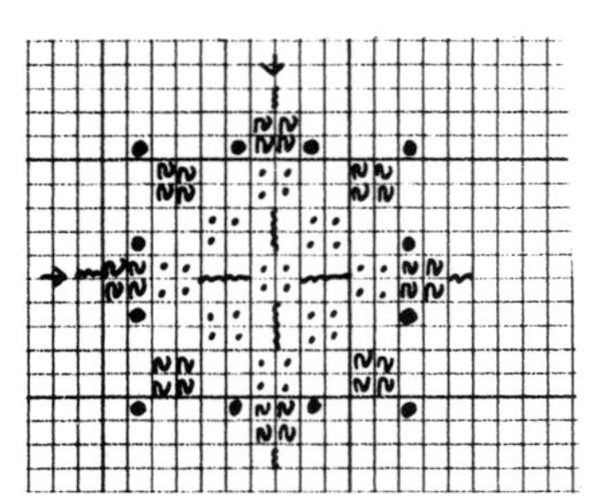

Snowflake ▴

16 stitches by 16 stitches

BACK-STITCH	CROSS-STITCH	DMC #	
	N	959	Aqua
∿∿∿	●	995	Dark Electric Blue
	·	996	Medium Electric Blue

Bell Border ▾

21-stitch repeat by 24 stitches

	DMC #	
N	517	Medium Wedgwod Blue
/	518	Light Wedgwood Blue
I	606	Bright Orange Red
O	742	Light Tangerine
◣	815	Medium Garnet Red
S	911	Medium Emerald Green

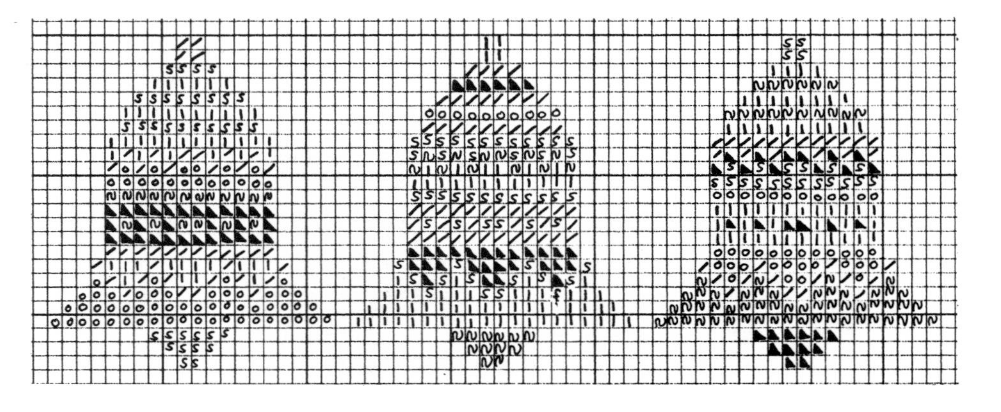

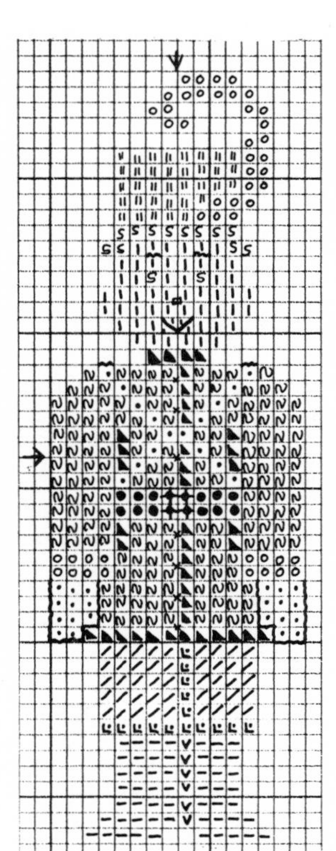

◂ *Toy Soldier*

16 stitches by 50 stitches

FRENCH KNOT	BACK-STITCH	CROSS-STITCH	DMC #	
		◣	304	Medium Christmas Red
	~~	●	310	Black
		I	353	Peach
		o	444	Dark Lemon Yellow
		S	518	Light Wedgwood Blue
		II	519	Sky Blue
□	—	N	606	Bright Orange Red
		V	645	Very Dark Beaver Gray
		—	647	Medium Beaver Gray
		✦	742	Light Tangerine
		L	910	Dark Emerald Green
		/	913	Medium Nile Green
		•		White

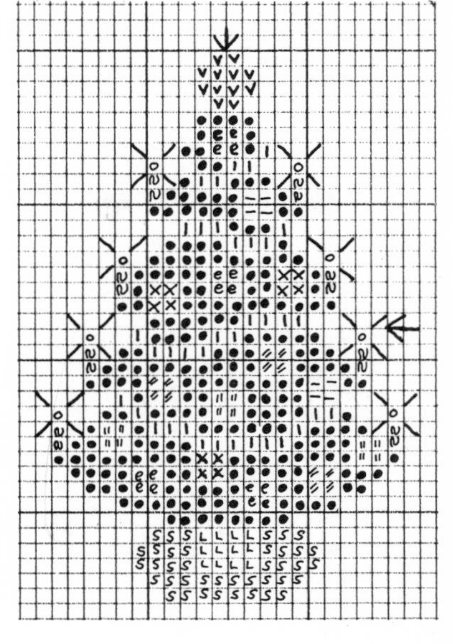

Tree with Candles ▸

24 stitches by 36 stitches

BACK-STITCH	CROSS-STITCH	DMC #	
	L	301	Medium Mahogany
	o	444	Dark Lemon Yellow
	N	666	Bright Christmas Red
	V	725	Topaz
—	—	741	Medium Tangerine
	e	742	Light Tangerine
	I	747	Very Light Sky Blue
	II	894	Very Light Carnation
	●	904	Very Dark Parrot Green
	//	954	Nile Green
	S	996	Medium Electric Blue
	X	3608	Fuchsia

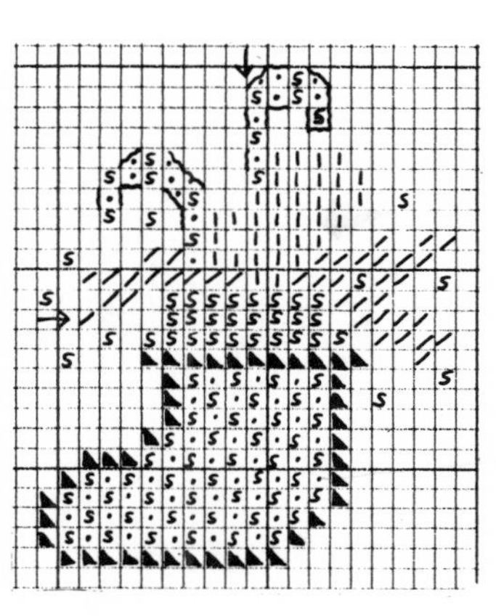

Stocking ▸

20 stitches by 25 stitches

BACK-STITCH	CROSS-STITCH	DMC #	
~~	S	666	Bright Christmas Red
	I	702	Kelly Green
	◣	815	Medium Garnet Red
	•		White

Duck ▸

26 stitches by 24 stitches

BACK-STITCH	CROSS-STITCH	DMC #	
	V	598	Light Turquoise
	N	606	Bright Orange Red
	/	702	Kelly Green
	I	742	Light Tangerine
~~		927	Medium Gray Blue
	•		White

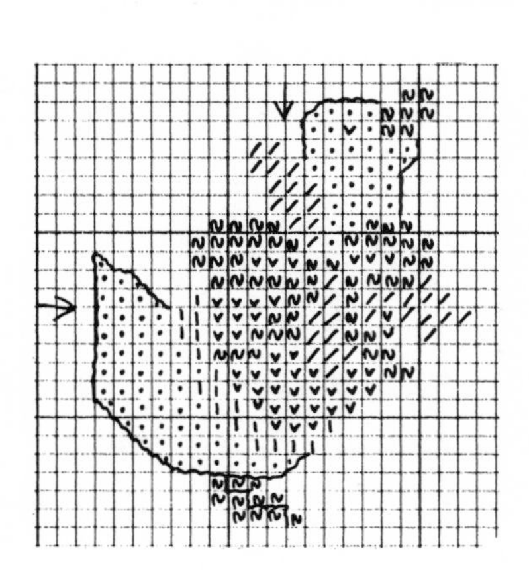

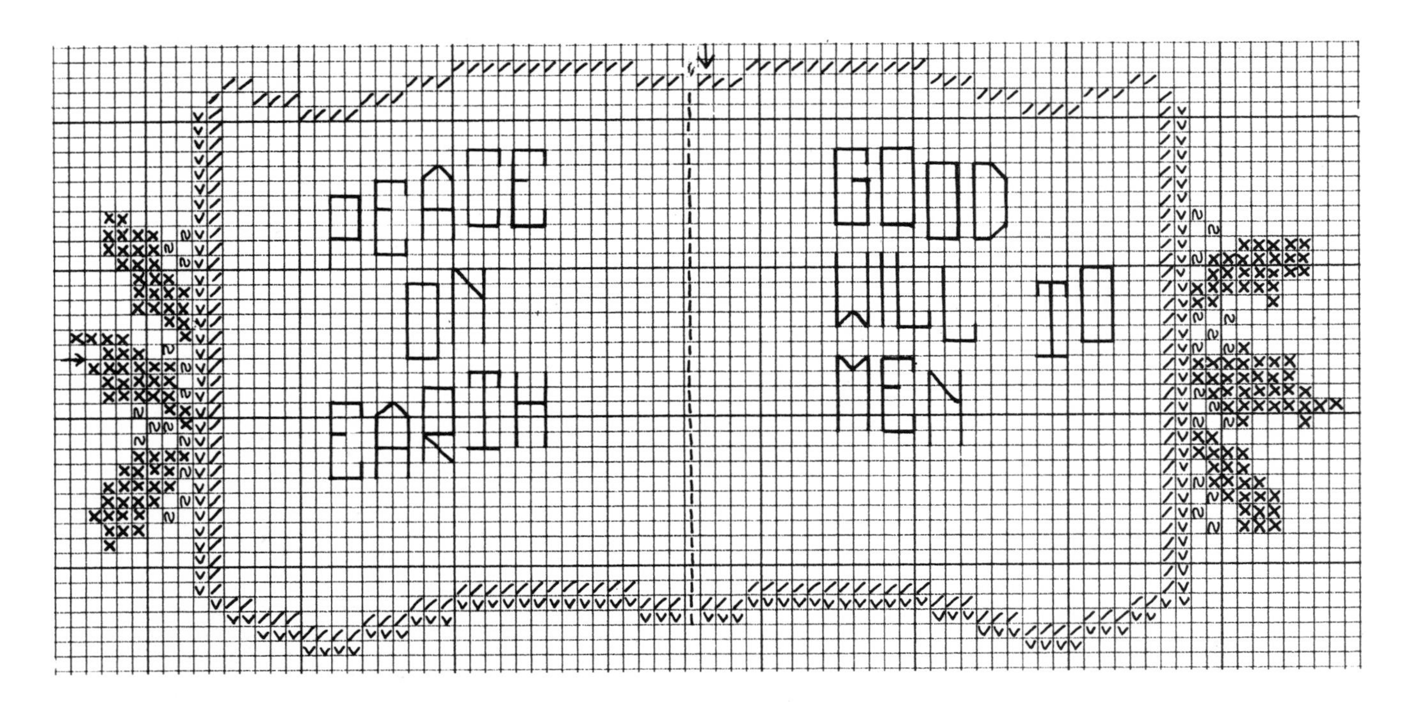

Peace on Earth ▲

83 stitches by 40 stitches

BACK-STITCH	CROSS-STITCH	DMC #	
	I	415	Pearl Gray
	S	666	Bright Christmas Red
	/	725	Topaz
	V	783	Christmas Gold
——		796	Dark Royal Blue
	X	910	Dark Emerald Green

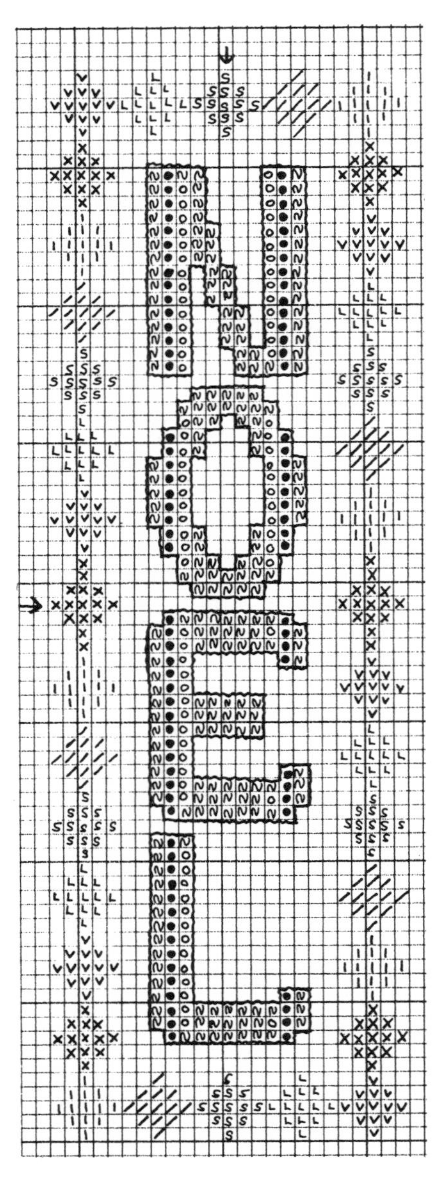

Noel ▸

25 stitches by 77 stitches

BACK-STITCH	CROSS-STITCH	DMC #	
	S	209	Dark Lavender
	L	603	Cranberry
	V	606	Bright Orange Red
	N	666	Bright Christmas Red
	/	704	Bright Chartreuse
	I	740	Tangerine
	o	742	Light Tangerine
~~	●	910	Dark Emerald Green
	X	996	Medium Electric Blue

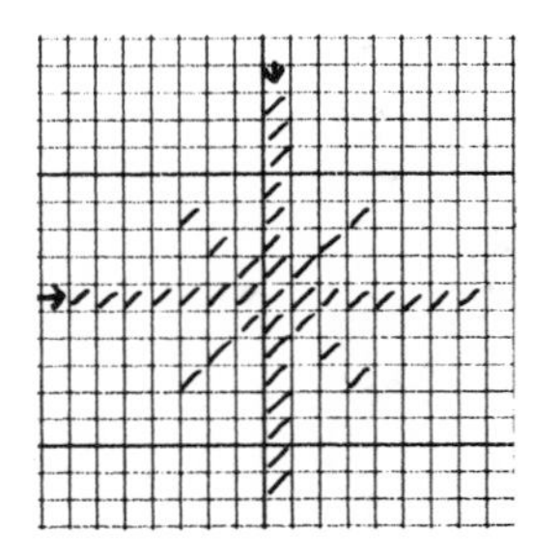

◂ Snowflake

15 stitches by 15 stitches

	DMC #	
/	827	Very Light Blue

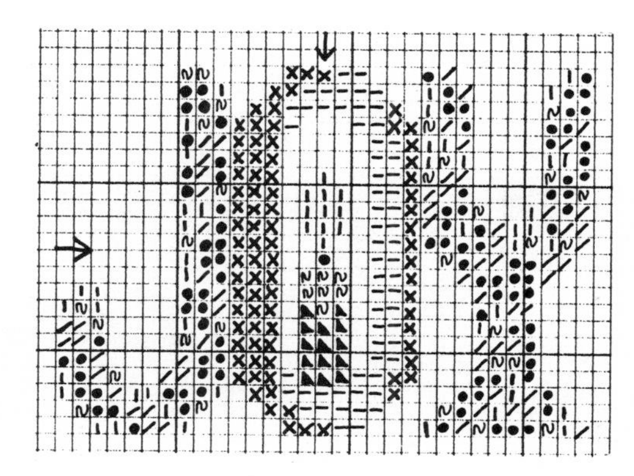

Joy ▲

31 stitches by 22 stitches

	DMC #	
◫	444	Dark Lemon Yellow
◫	606	Bright Orange Red
◣	666	Bright Christmas Red
●	910	Dark Emerald Green
◩	913	Medium Nile Green
☒	995	Dark Electric Blue
⊟	996	Medium Electric Blue

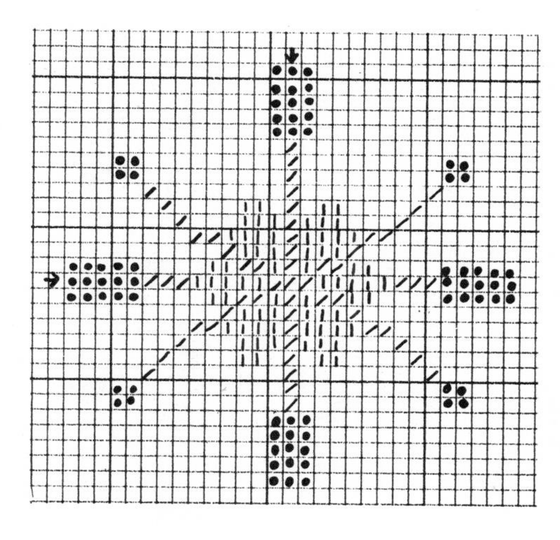

Snowflake ▲

29 stitches by 29 stitches

	DMC #	
◩	341	Light Lilac
◫	518	Light Wedgwood Blue
●	793	Medium Cornflower Blue

Tree ▼

33 stitches by 55 stitches

BACK-STITCH	CROSS-STITCH	DMC #	
	●	580	Dark Moss Green
	≈	666	Bright Christmas Red
〰	◩	828	Very Pale Blue
	·		White

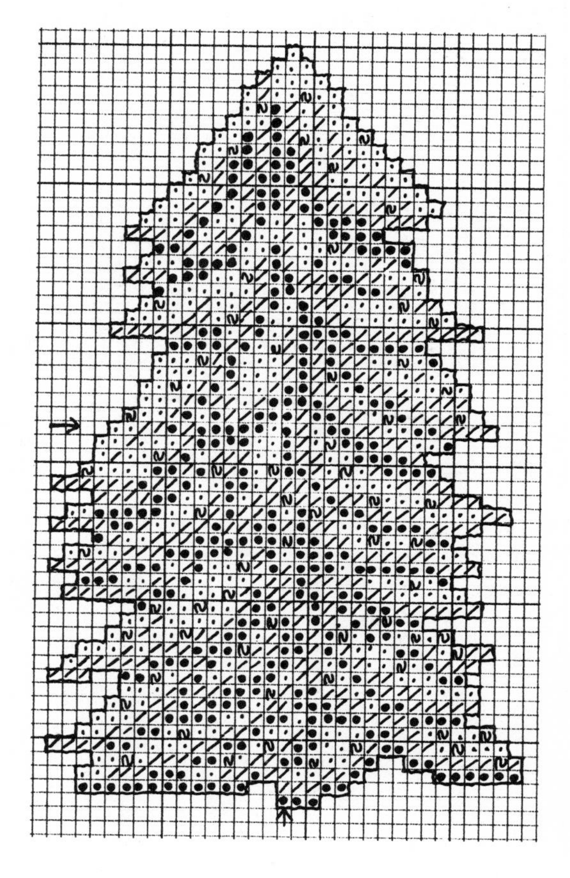

Ornament ▼

19 stitches by 17 stitches

	DMC #	
·	444	Dark Lemon Yellow
◫	606	Bright Orange Red
≈	666	Bright Christmas Red
◩	704	Bright Chartreuse
●	816	Garnet Red
V	996	Medium Electric Blue

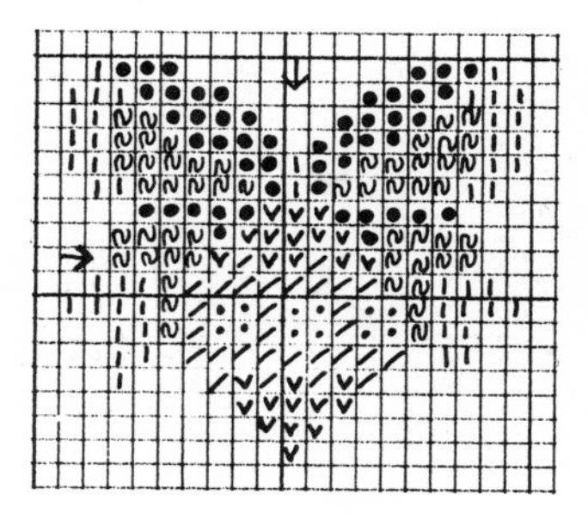

Stained Glass Alphabet

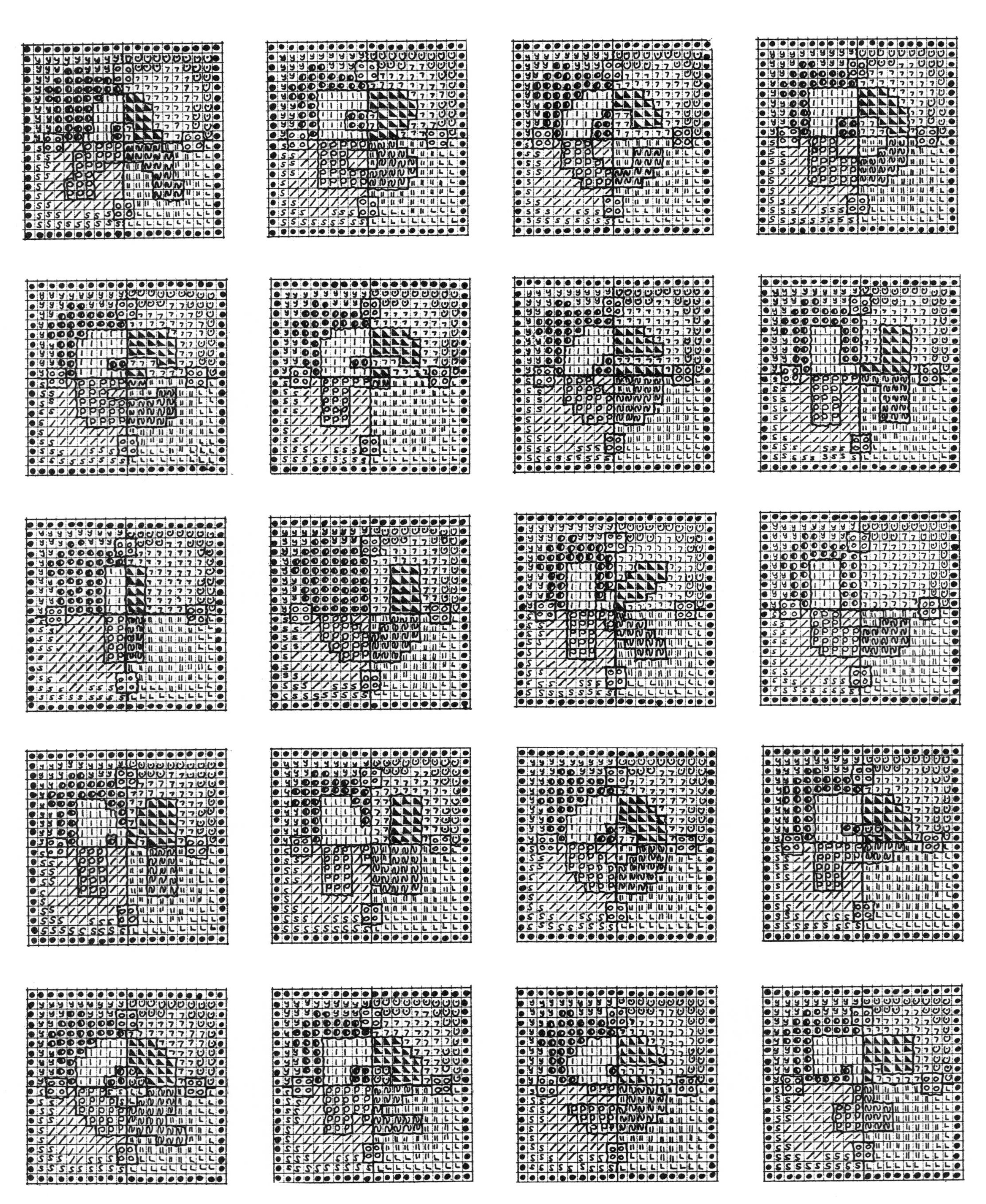

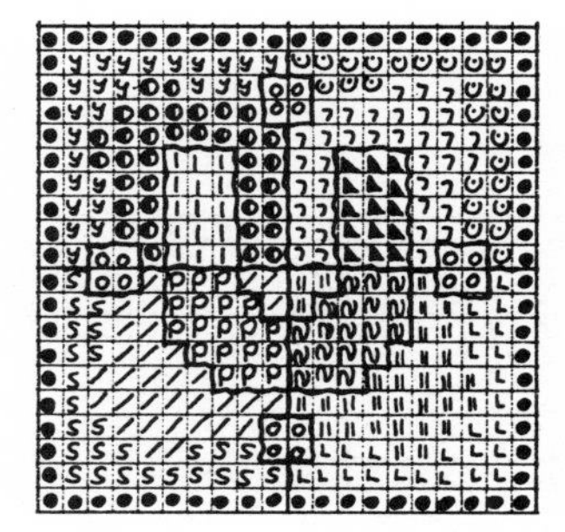
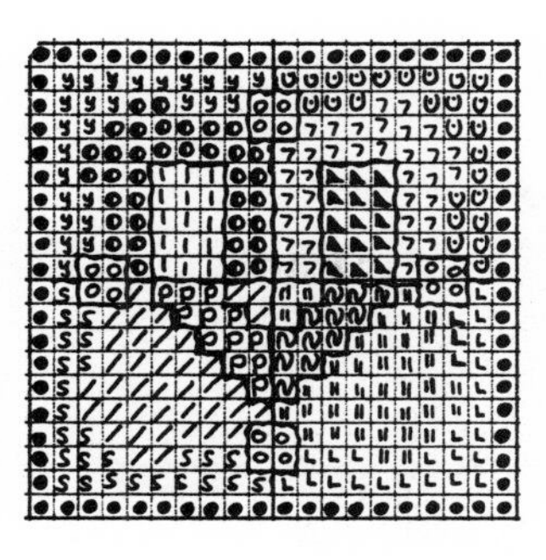

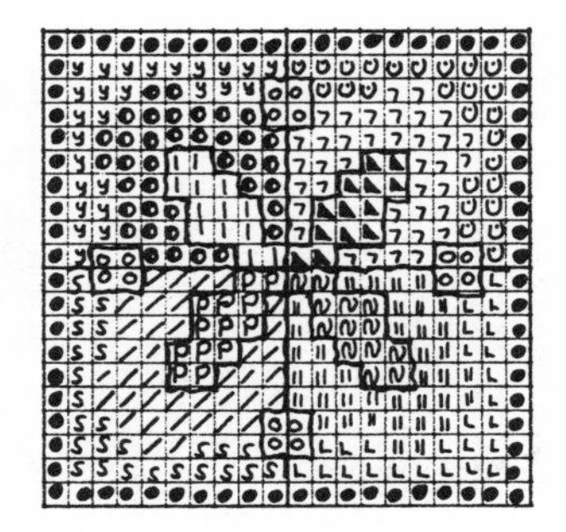
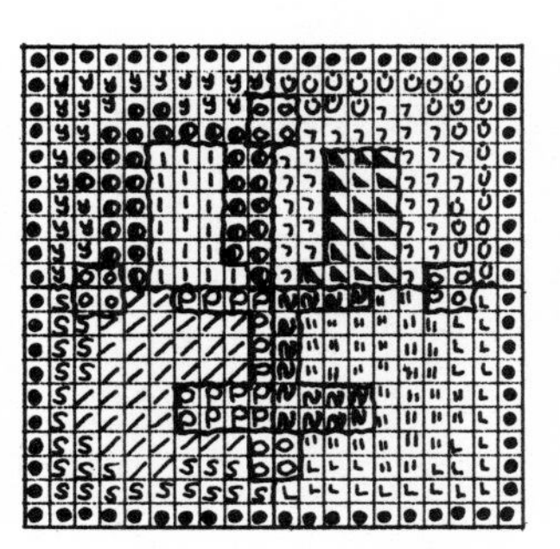
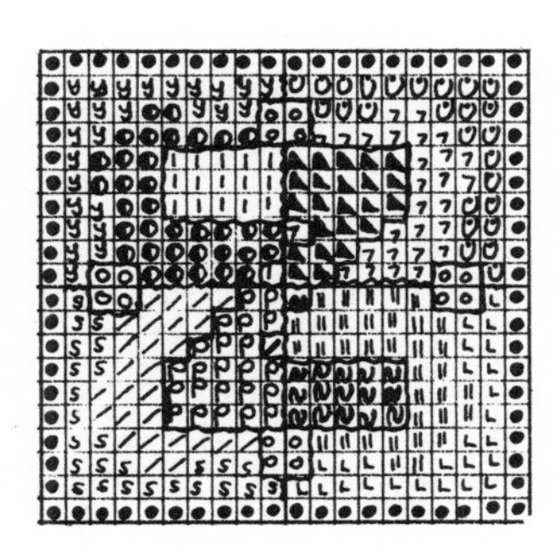

Stained Glass Alphabet ▲

Each letter, 20 stitches by 20 stitches

BACK-STITCH	CROSS-STITCH	DMC #	
	P	304	Medium Christmas Red
∿∿∿	●	336	Navy Blue
	O	444	Dark Lemon Yellow
	y	517	Medium Wedgwood Blue
	I	606	Bright Orange Red
	N	666	Bright Christmas Red
	◐	701	Light Christmas Green
	/	703	Chartreuse
	L	806	Dark Peacock Blue
	♥	816	Garnet Red
	II	912	Light Emerald Green
	7	913	Medium Nile Green
	S	943	Medium Aquamarine
	ʊ	995	Dark Electric Blue

Drum ▸

36 stitches by 31 stitches

	DMC #	
/	415	Pearl Gray
I	606	Bright Orange Red
//	725	Topaz
S	781	Dark Topaz
V	783	Christmas Gold
X	912	Light Emerald Green
•		White

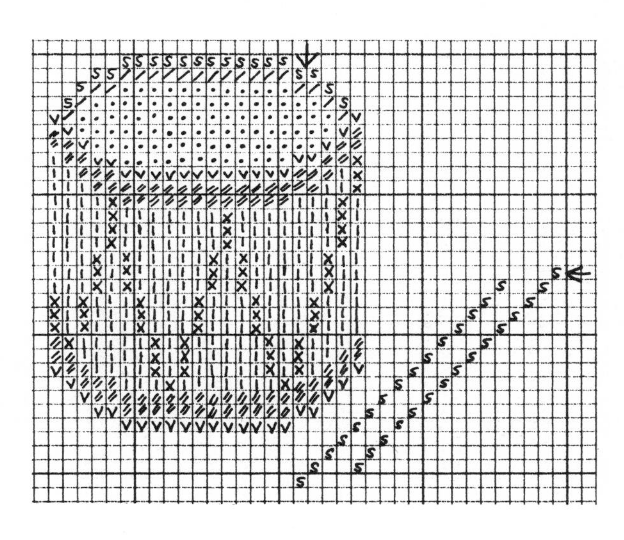

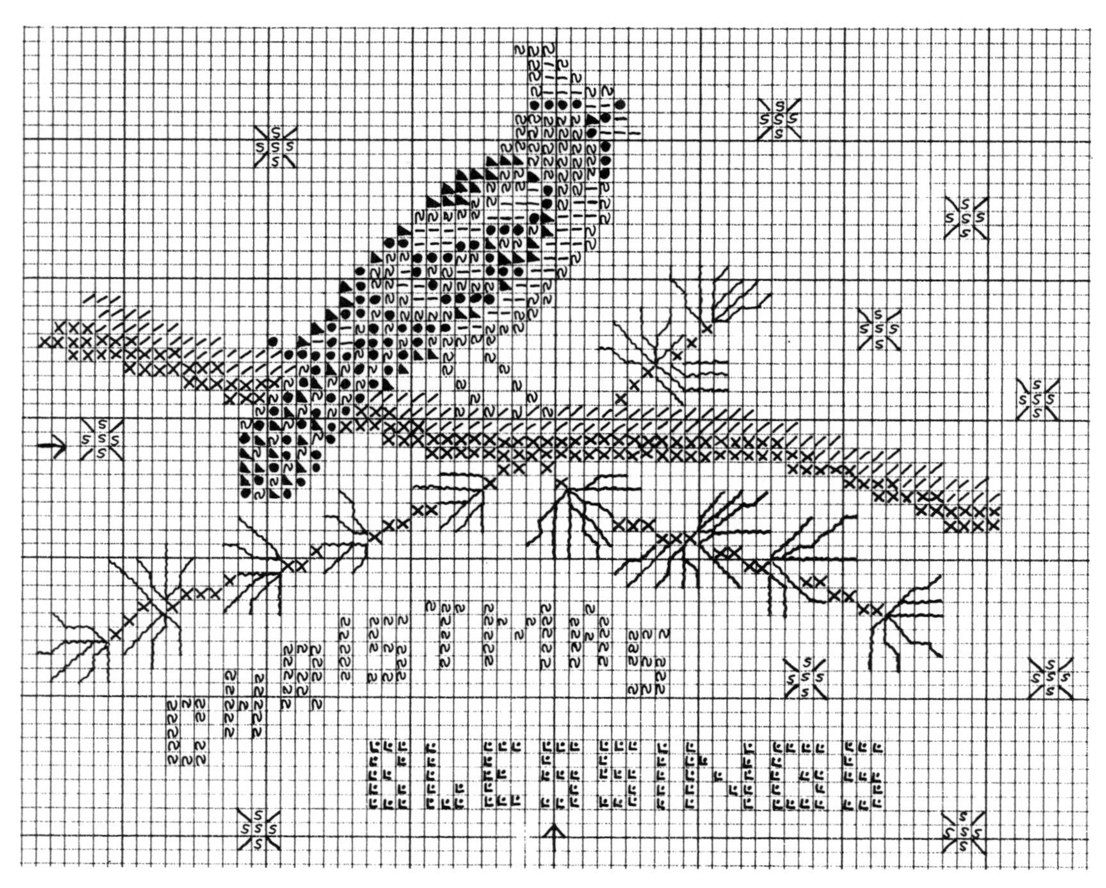

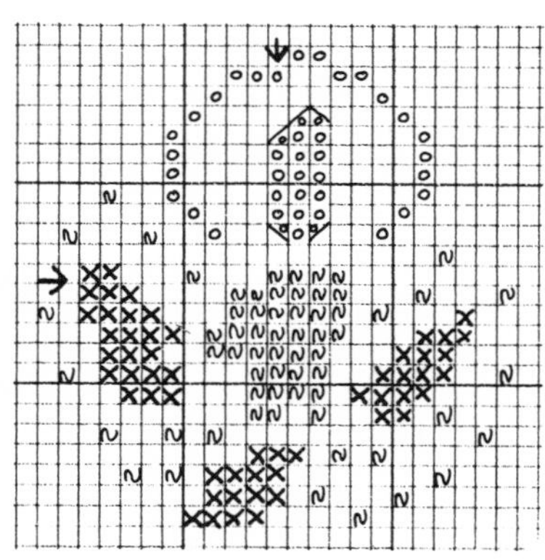

Cardinal ▲

72 stitches by 58 stitches

BACK-STITCH	CROSS-STITCH	DMC #	
	●	310	Black
	−	352	Light Coral
~~		581	Moss Green
	~	666	Bright Christmas Red
	◣	815	Medium Garnet Red
——	S	827	Very Light Blue
	×	975	Dark Golden Brown
	/	976	Medium Golden Brown
	L	995	Dark Electric Blue

Candle ▲

23 stitches by 25 stitches

BACK-STITCH	CROSS-STITCH	DMC #	
	~	606	Bright Orange Red
——	o	742	Light Tangerine
	×	911	Medium Emerald Green

Tree Border ▼

7-stitch by 8-stitch repeat

	DMC #	
●	400	Dark Mahogany
/	910	Dark Emerald Green

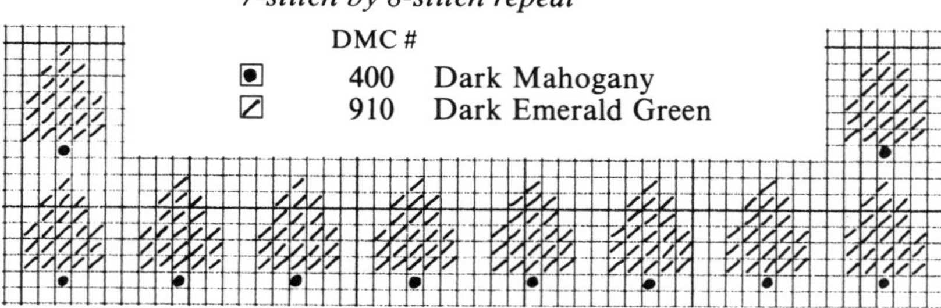

Happy Holidays Wreath ▲

67 stitches by 92 stitches

BACK-STITCH	CROSS-STITCH	DMC #	
	P	340	Lilac
	6	606	Bright Orange Red
	I	608	Bright Orange
∿∿∿	N	666	Bright Christmas Red
	◐	699	Christmas Green
	S	701	Light Christmas Green
	/	704	Bright Chartreuse
	C	740	Tangerine
	·	743	Dark Yellow
	◣	816	Garnet Red
	L	827	Very Light Blue
	●	995	Dark Electric Blue

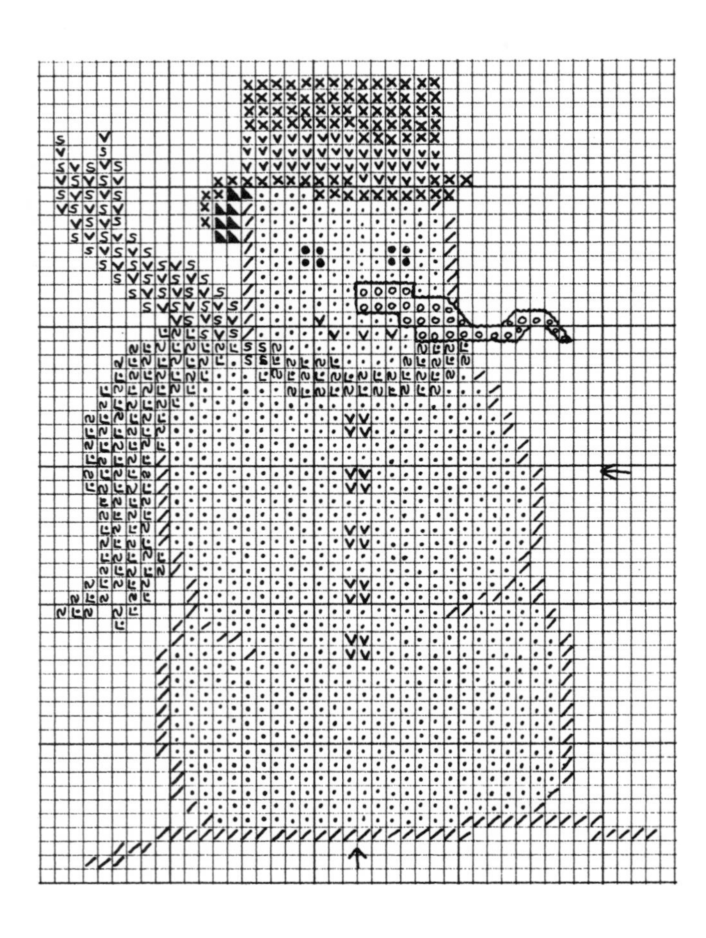

Snowman

42 stitches by 57 stitches

BACK-STITCH	CROSS-STITCH	DMC #	
	●	310	Black
	V	606	Bright Orange Red
	N	666	Bright Christmas Red
	/	827	Very Light Blue
	◣	909	Very Dark Emerald Green
	X	912	Light Emerald Green
	L	995	Dark Electric Blue
	S	996	Medium Electric Blue
~~	O	3341	Light Melon
	·		White

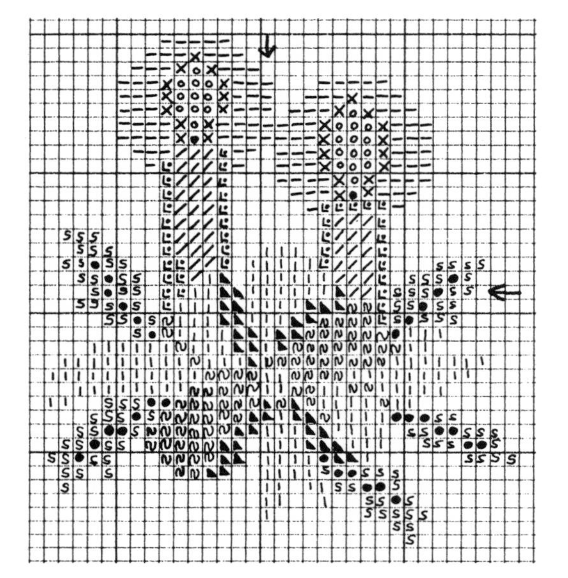

Candles and Holly

33 stitches by 37 stitches

	DMC #	
I	606	Bright Orange Red
N	666	Bright Christmas Red
–	741	Medium Tangerine
O	743	Dark Yellow
L	806	Dark Peacock Blue
/	807	Peacock Blue
◣	815	Medium Garnet Red
●	909	Very Dark Emerald Green
S	911	Medium Emerald Green
X	947	Burnt Orange

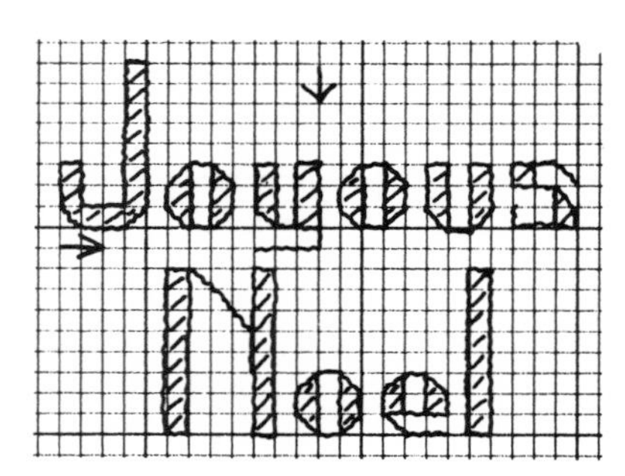

Joyous Noel

24 stitches by 18 stitches

BACK-STITCH	CROSS-STITCH	DMC #	
~~	/	666	Bright Christmas Red

Christmas Rose

33 stitches by 21 stitches

	DMC #	
/	415	Pearl Gray
O	444	Dark Lemon Yellow
●	469	Avocado Green
X	701	Light Christmas Green
·		White

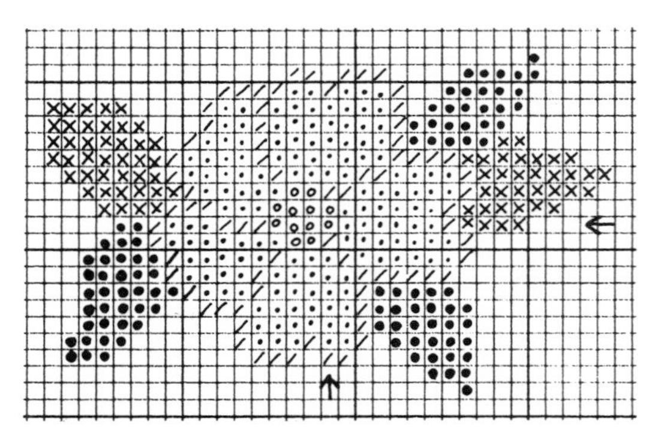

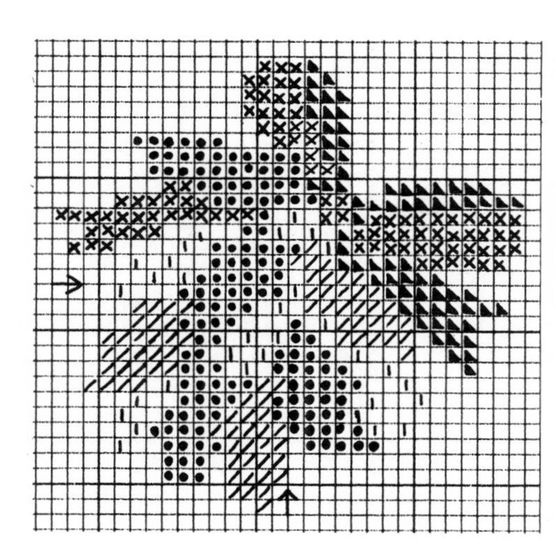

◂ *Spray of Holly*

30 stitches by 30 stitches

	DMC #	
●	580	Dark Moss Green
/	581	Moss Green
I	606	Bright Orange Red
◣	995	Dark Electric Blue
X	996	Medium Electric Blue

Tiny Santa ▸

24 stitches by 34 stitches

BACK-STITCH	CROSS-STITCH	DMC #	
	−	353	Peach
	V	603	Cranberry
	I	666	Bright Christmas Red
——		718	Plum
	/	747	Very Light Sky Blue
	·		White

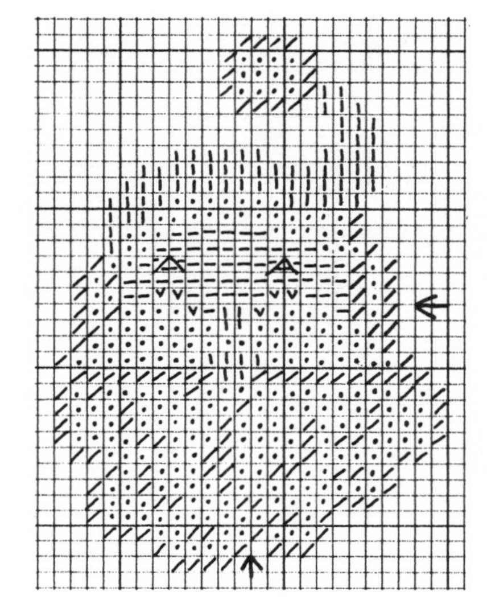

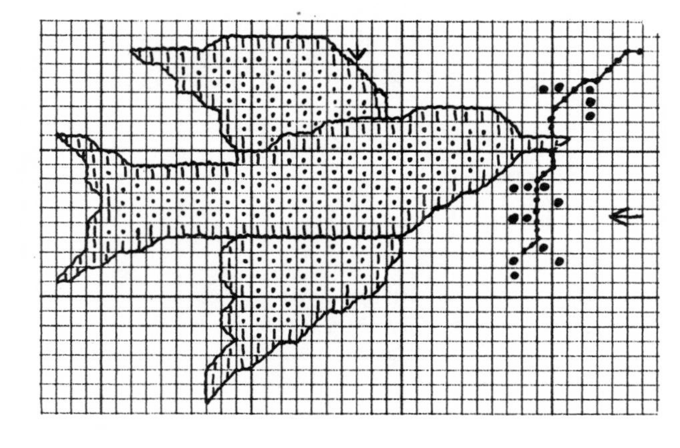

◂ *Dove*

38 stitches by 25 stitches

BACK-STITCH	CROSS-STITCH	DMC #	
~~	I	647	Medium Beaver Gray
-•-•-		910	Dark Emerald Green
	●	911	Medium Emerald Green
	·		White

Mrs. Santa and Heart ▸

31 stitches by 28 stitches

	DMC #	
◣	310	Black
−	353	Peach
I	666	Bright Christmas Red
o	725	Topaz
X	910	Dark Emerald Green
●	995	Dark Electric Blue
/	996	Medium Electric Blue
·		White

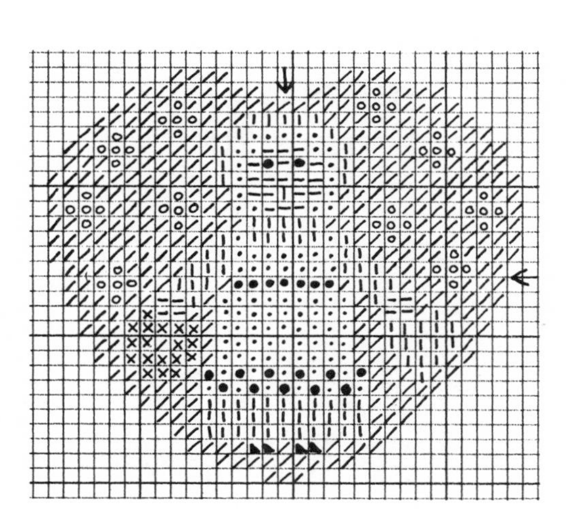

◂ *Tree with Candles*

41 stitches by 45 stitches

	DMC #	
◣	210	Medium Lavender
■	608	Bright Orange
☒	666	Bright Christmas Red
S	740	Tangerine
●	743*	Dark Yellow
⁄	910	Dark Emerald Green
I	955	Light Nile Green
P	996	Medium Electric Blue

*If desired, replace 743 Dark Yellow with Balger #8 braid, Gold #002.

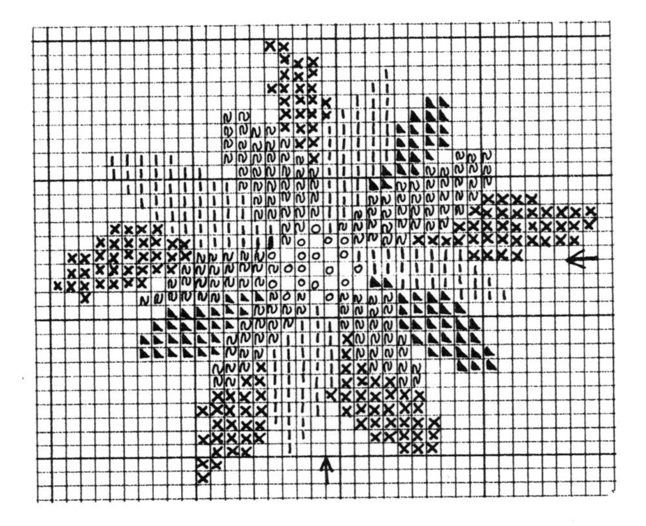

Poinsettia ▴

38 stitches by 32 stitches

	DMC #	
I	606	Bright Orange Red
N	666	Bright Christmas Red
O	725	Topaz
◣	816	Garnet Red
☒	910	Dark Emerald Green

Stocking Border ▾

14-stitch repeat by 26 stitches

	DMC #	
N	304	Medium Christmas Red
⁄•	800	Pale Delft Blue
●	911	Medium Emerald Green
⁄	995	Dark Electric Blue
·		White

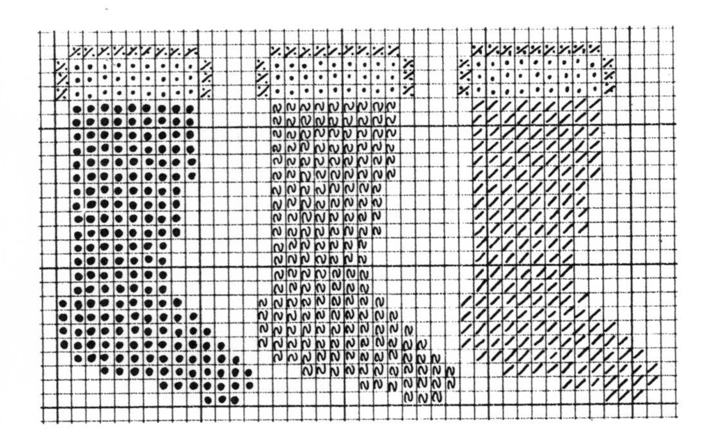

A Joyful Christmas ▸

49 stitches by 17 stitches

BACK-STITCH	CROSS-STITCH	DMC #	
─•─•─	I	606	Bright Orange Red
∿∿∿	⁄	912	Light Emerald Green

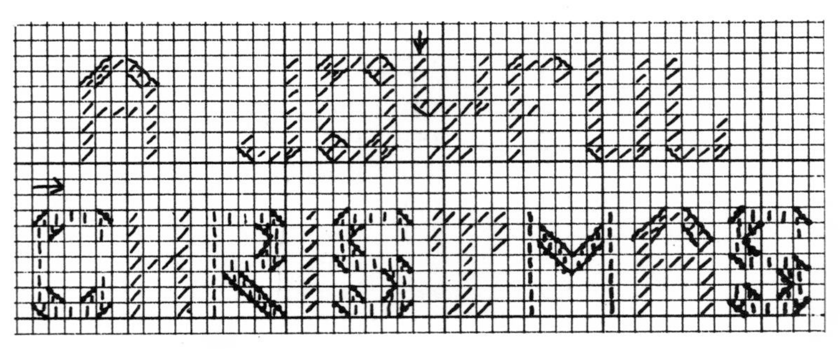

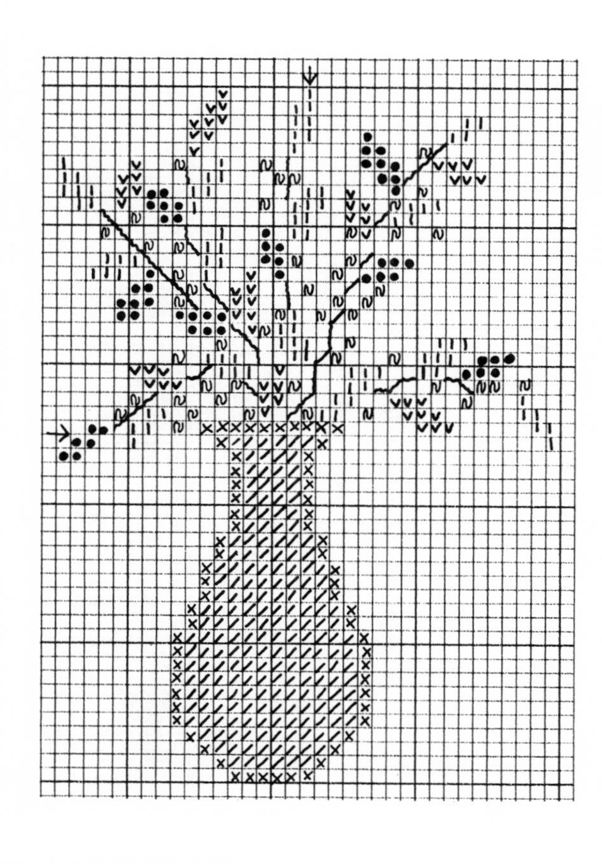

◂ *Vase of Berries*

36 stitches by 50 stitches

BACK-STITCH	CROSS-STITCH	DMC #	
	V	469	Avocado Green
	N	666	Bright Christmas Red
	X	799	Medium Delft Blue
	/	809	Delft Blue
	I	911	Medium Emerald Green
~~	●	986	Dark Forest Green

Christmas Mouse ▸

32 stitches by 37 stitches

FRENCH KNOT	BACK-STITCH	CROSS-STITCH	DMC #	
×		●	310	Black
	~~		318	Light Steel Gray
		/	415	Pearl Gray
	——	I	606	Bright Orange Red
		V	754	Light Peach
		·		White

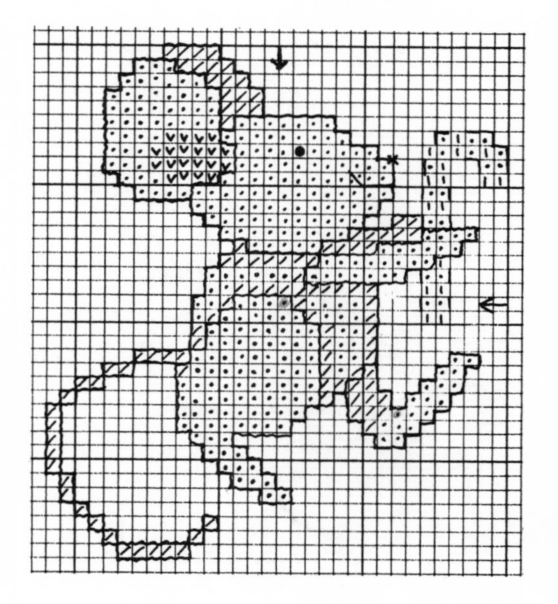

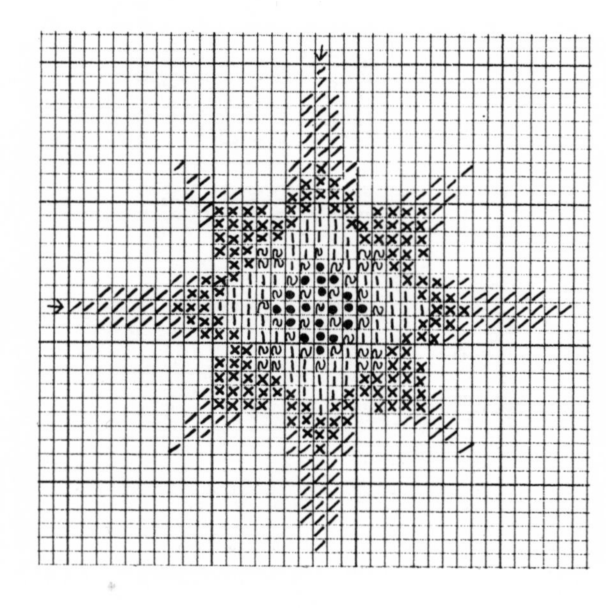

◂ *Christmas Star*

35 stitches by 35 stitches

	DMC #	
N	606	Bright Orange Red
I	726	Light Topaz
/	828	Very Pale Blue
X	911	Medium Emerald Green
●	995	Dark Electric Blue

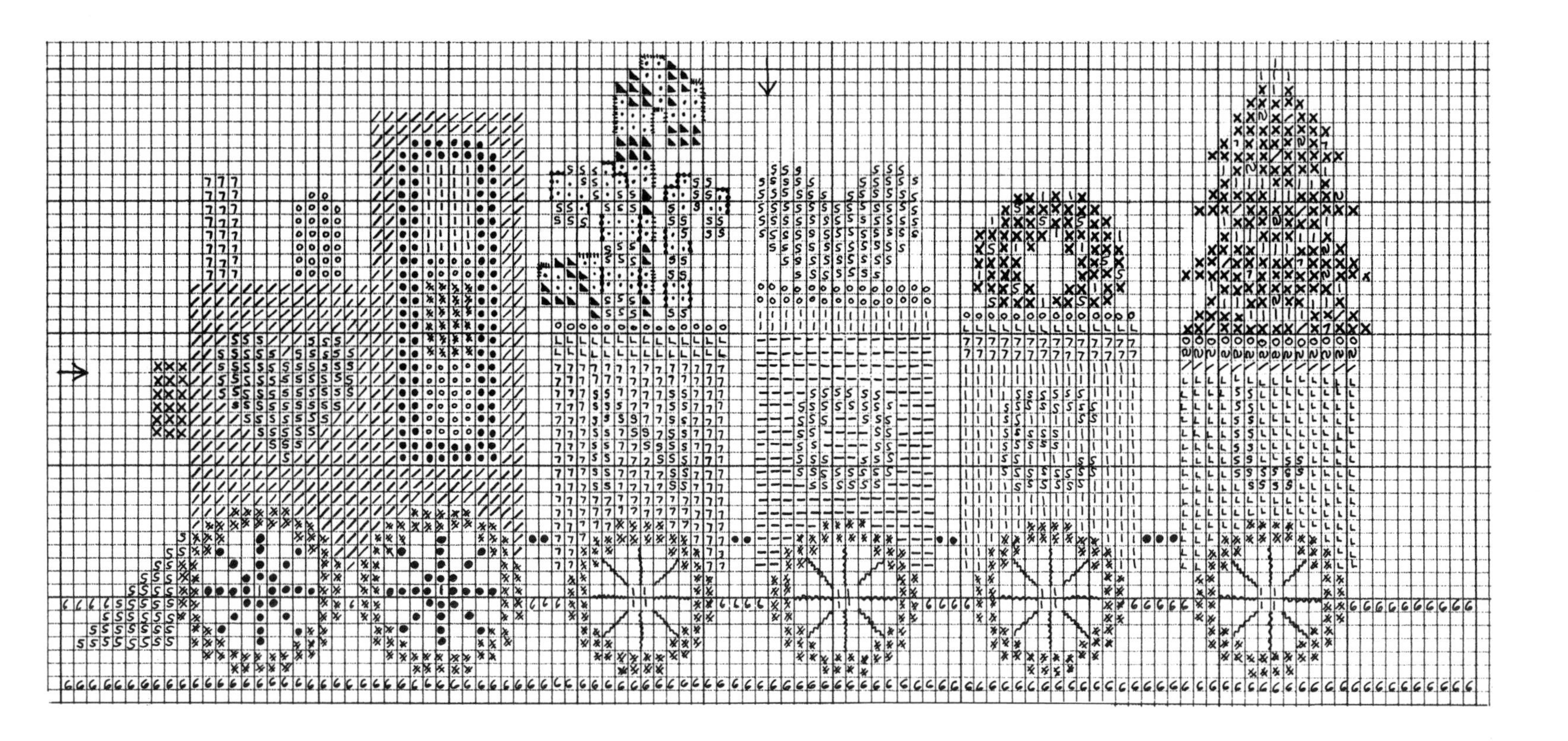

Christmas Train ▲

110 stitches by 47 stitches

BACK-STITCH	CROSS-STITCH	DMC #	
	6	318	Light Steel Gray
ıııııı	◣	498	Dark Christmas Red
	L	518	Light Wedgwood Blue
	–	553	Medium Violet
•—•—•	S	606	Bright Orange Red
	/	740	Tangerine
	I	743	Dark Yellow
~~	●	824	Very Dark Blue
	X	910	Dark Emerald Green
	✱	911	Medium Emerald Green
	O	954	Nile Green
	7	996	Medium Electric Blue
	•		White

▼ Snowflake Border

12-stitch repeat by 9 stitches

	DMC #	
X	813	Light Blue
/	827	Very Light Blue

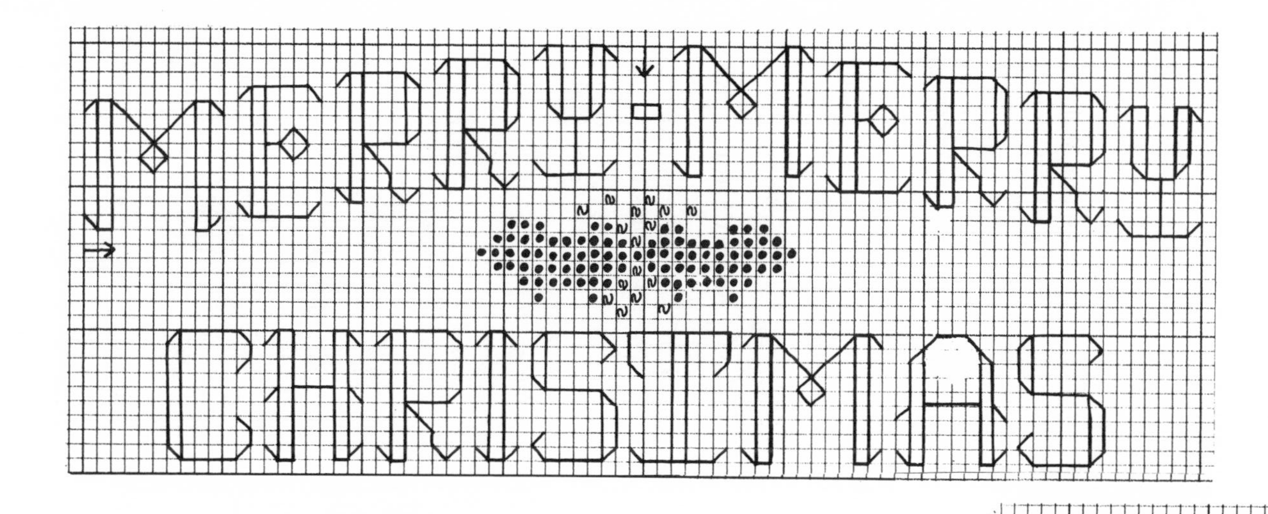

▼ *Noel*

60 stitches by 25 stitches

	DMC #	
|	666	Bright Christmas Red
–	815	Medium Garnet Red
/	910	Dark Emerald Green
●	995	Dark Electric Blue

Merry, Merry Christmas ▲

80 stitches by 29 stitches

BACK-STITCH	CROSS-STITCH	DMC #	
—	≈	666	Bright Christmas Red
	●	910	Dark Emerald Green

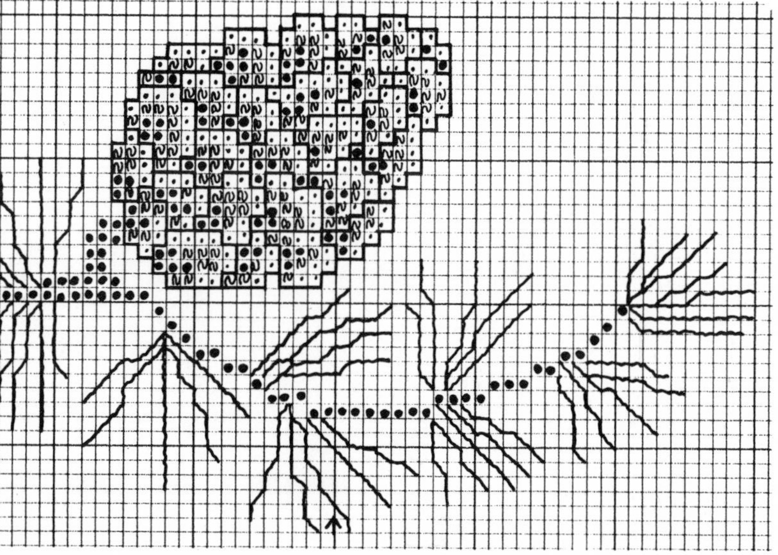

◂ *Pine Branch*

60 stitches by 36 stitches

BACK-STITCH	CROSS-STITCH	DMC #	
—	●	433	Medium Brown
	≈	435	Very Light Brown
	·	437	Light Tan
~~		700	Bright Christmas Green

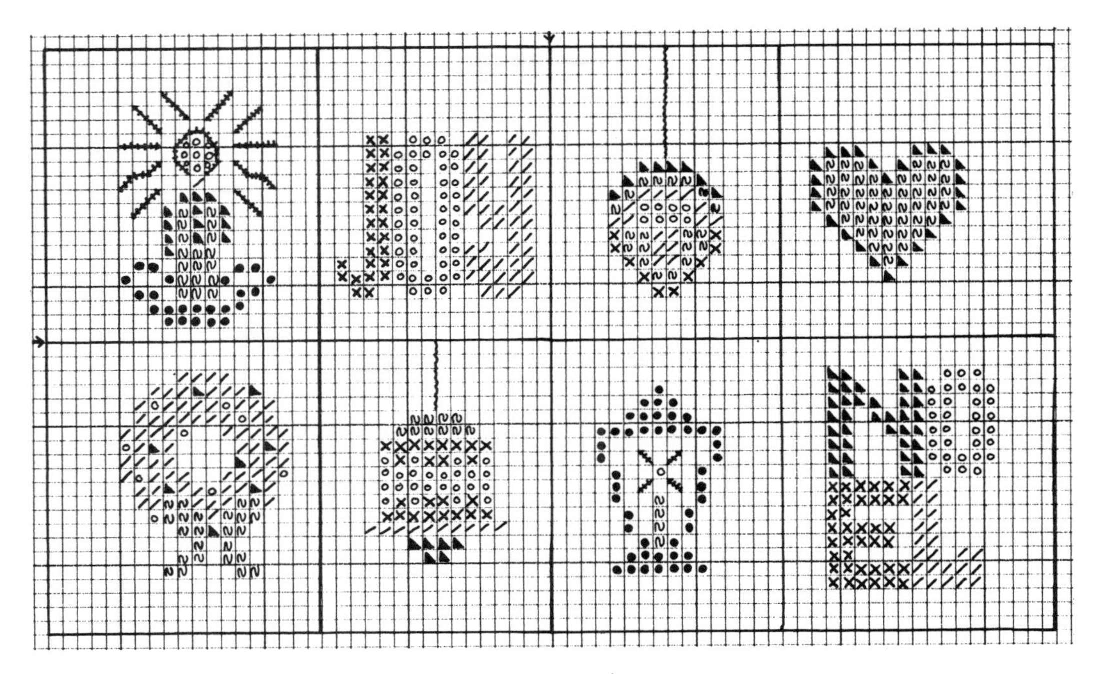

▲ *Christmas Card*

70 stitches by 42 stitches

BACK-STITCH	CROSS-STITCH	DMC #	
┼┼┼┼┼	◙	444	Dark Lemon Yellow
〰	≈	666	Bright Christmas Red
	⧄	702	Kelly Green
——	●	801	Dark Coffee Brown
	◣	815	Medium Garnet Red
	☒	895	Dark Christmas Green

◀ *Tree Frame*

45 stitches by 58 stitches

BACK-STITCH	CROSS-STITCH	DMC #	
	⫴	666	Bright Christmas Red
	◙	725	Topaz
〰	⧄	910	Dark Emerald Green
	●	920	Medium Copper

Wreath ▼

19 stitches by 19 stitches

BACK-STITCH	CROSS-STITCH	DMC #	
	◙	606	Bright Orange Red
	≈	742	Light Tangerine
	☒	911	Medium Emerald Green

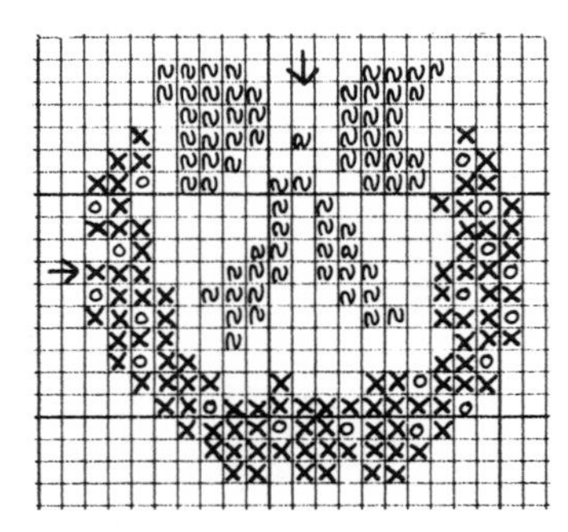

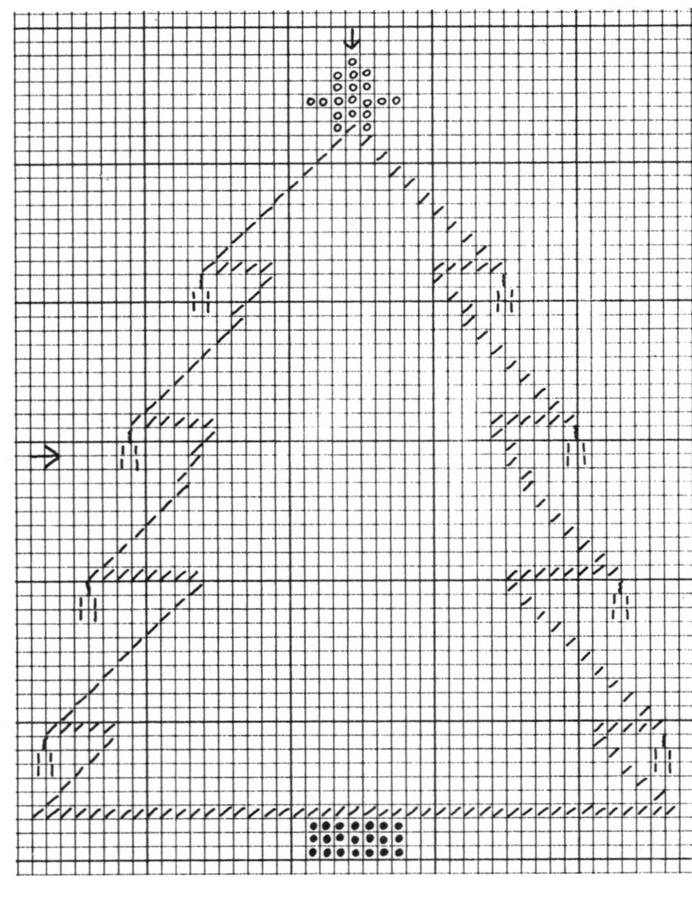

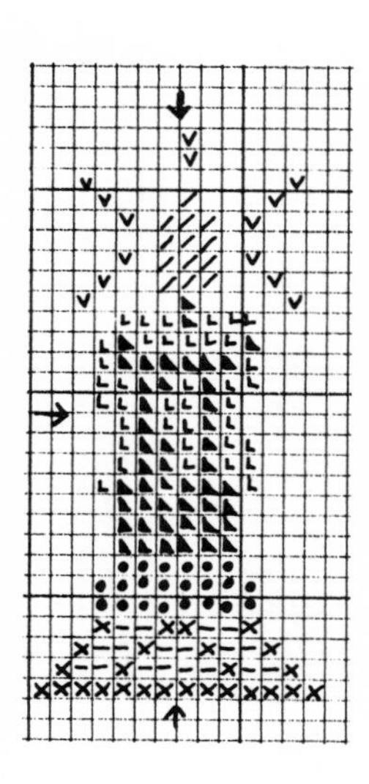

◂ Candle

14 stitches by 28 stitches

	DMC #	
●	517	Medium Wedgwood Blue
−	518	Light Wedgwood Blue
X	519	Sky Blue
◣	606	Bright Orange Red
L	608	Bright Orange
V	725	Topaz
/	726	Light Topaz

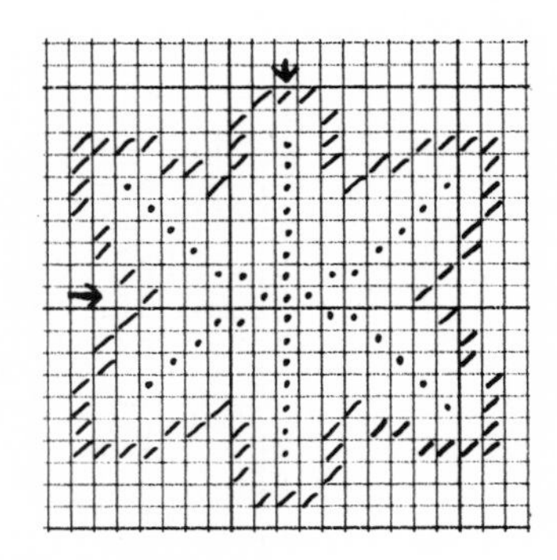

Snowflake ▴

19 stitches by 19 stitches

	DMC #	
/	813	Light Blue
•	827	Very Light Blue

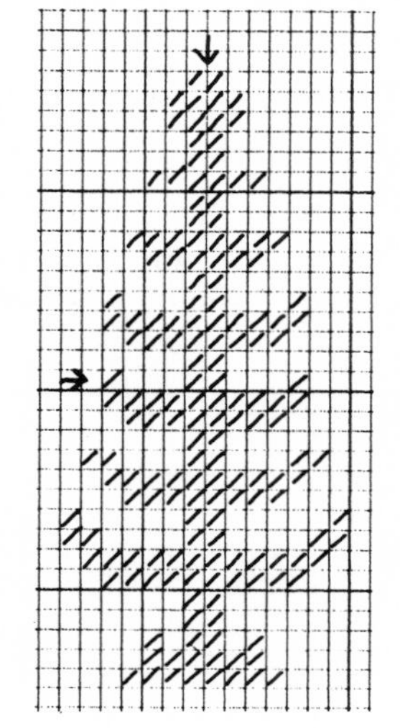

▾ Noel

10 stitches by 39 stitches

	DMC #	
I	813	Light Blue
●	825	Dark Blue
S	826	Medium Blue
/	827	Very Light Blue
•	828	Very Pale Blue

◂ Tree

13 stitches by 31 stitches

	DMC #	
/	912	Light Emerald Green

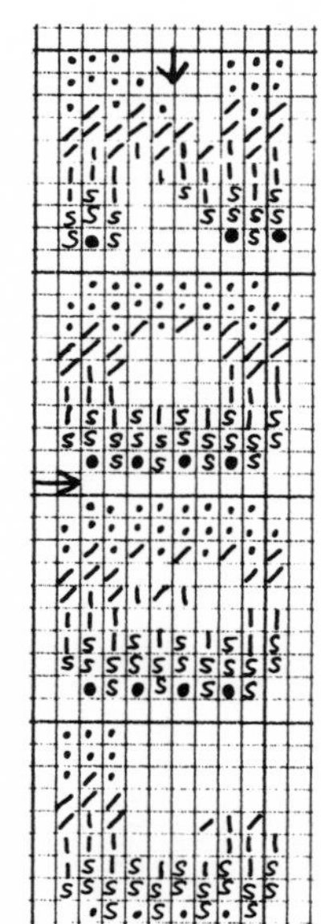

Joy ▸

10 stitches by 38 stitches

	DMC #	
N	606	Bright Orange Red
/	704	Bright Chartreuse
◣	824	Very Dark Blue
●	826	Medium Blue
X	912	Light Emerald Green

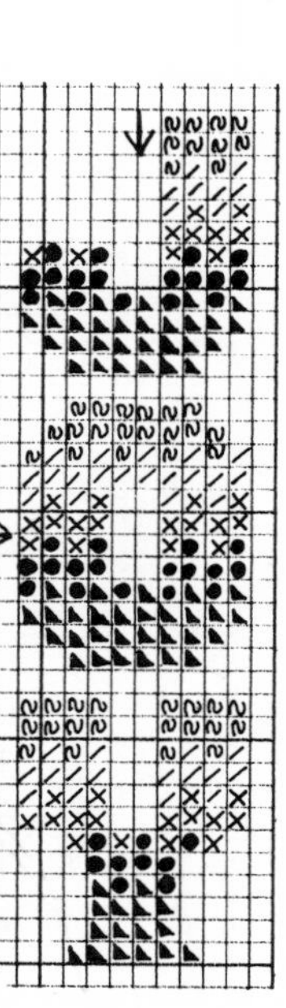

Tree Border ▾

10-stitch repeat by 15 stitches

	DMC #	
●	433	Medium Brown
I	444	Dark Lemon Yellow
O	741	Medium Tangerine
V	894	Very Light Carnation Pink
/	910	Dark Emerald Green
−	955	Light Nile Green
N	964	Light Aqua
•	996	Medium Electric Blue
S	3340	Melon

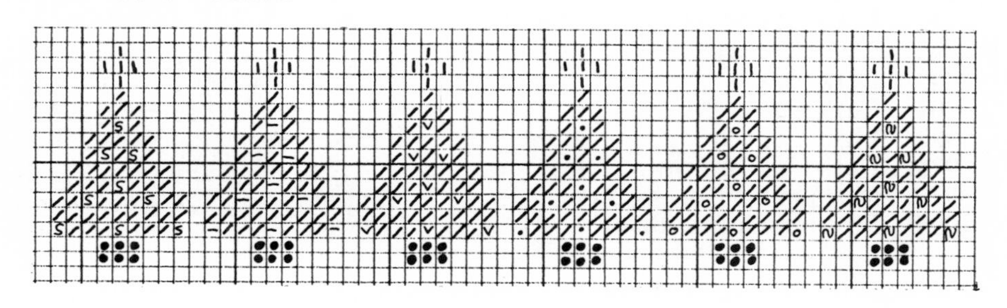

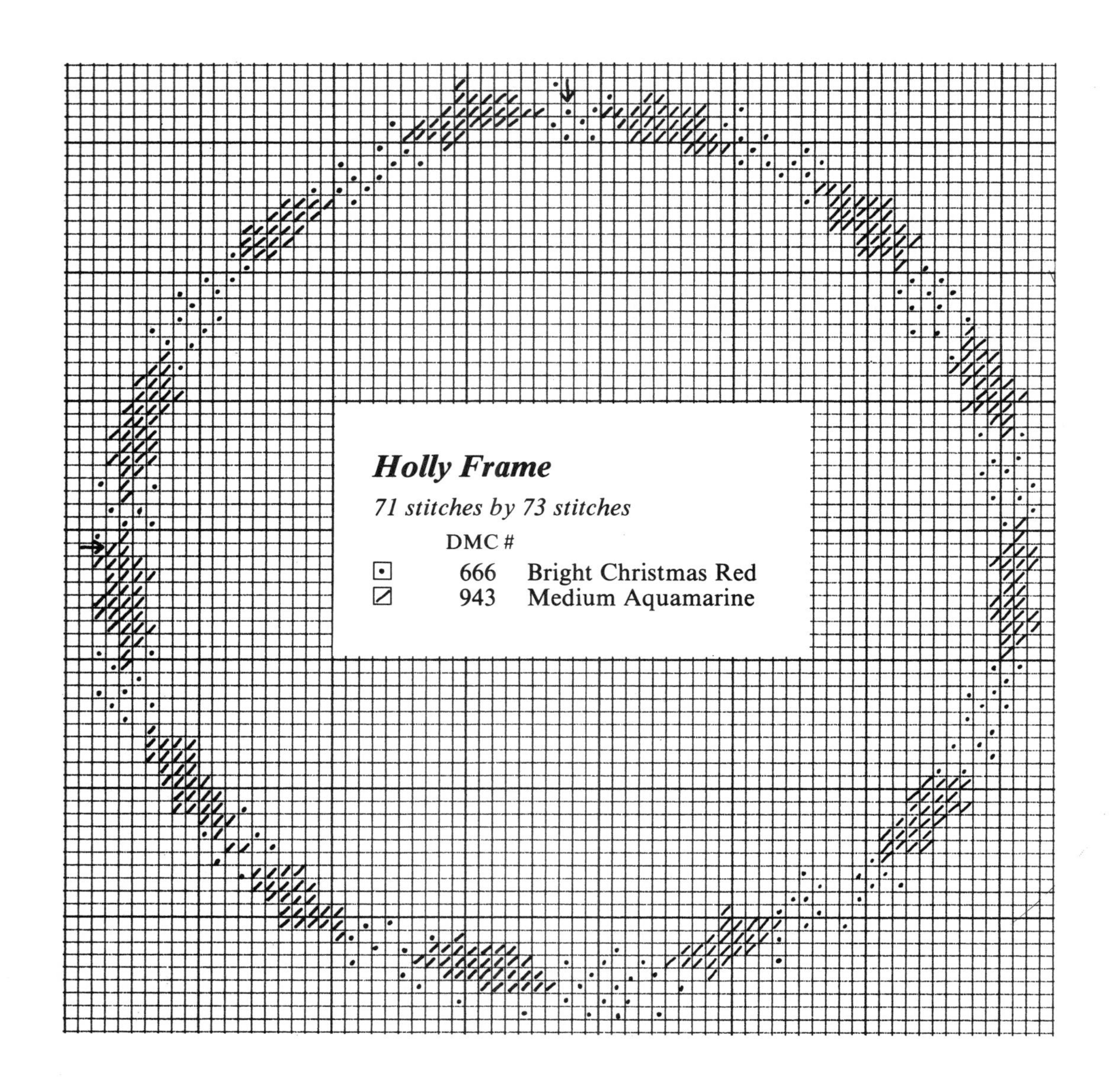

And the Stockings Were Hung . . . ▸

38 stitches by 37 stitches

BACK-STITCH	CROSS-STITCH	DMC #	
		310	Black
		433	Medium Brown
		435	Very Light Brown
		437	Light Tan
		666	Bright Christmas Red
		700	Bright Christmas Green
		704	Bright Chartreuse
		740	Tangerine
		742	Light Tangerine
		743	Dark Yellow
		801	Dark Coffee Brown
		922	Light Copper
		975	Dark Golden Brown
		976	Medium Golden Brown
		996	Medium Electric Blue

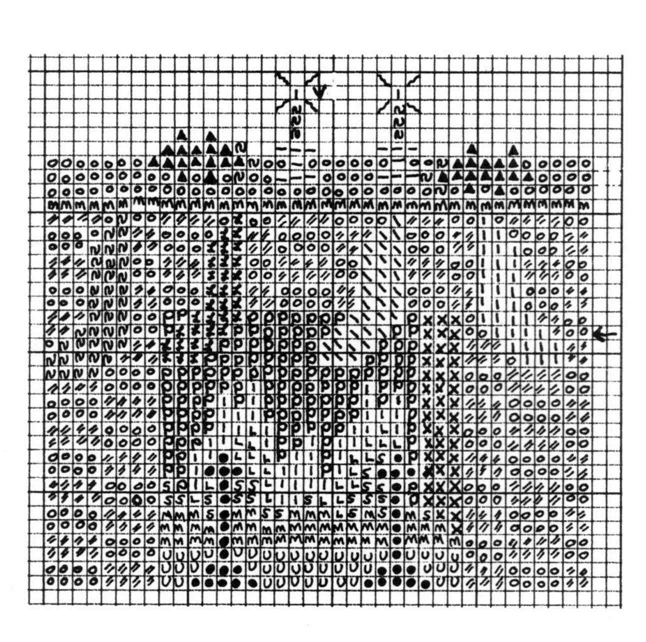

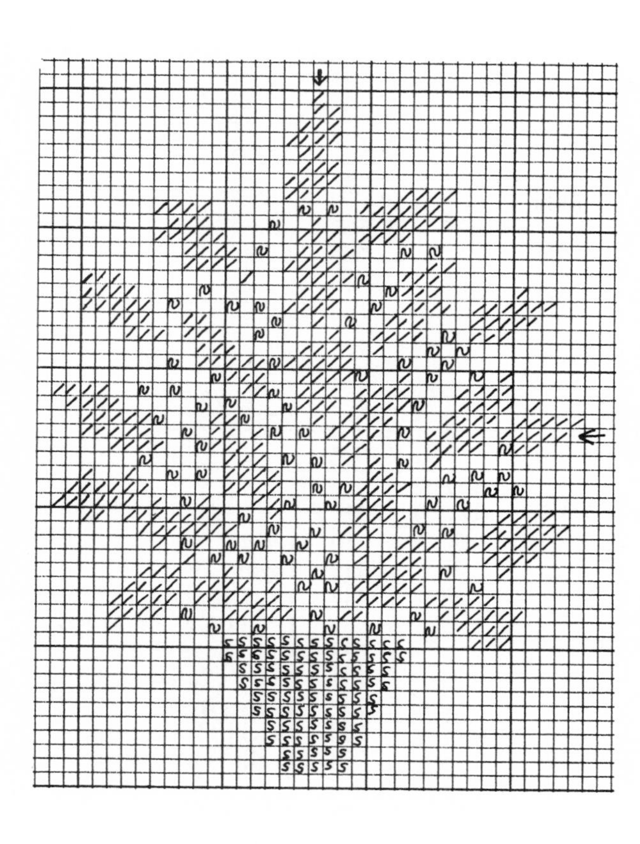

Pot of Holly

37 stitches by 49 stitches

DMC #	
400	Dark Mahogany
666	Bright Christmas Red
910	Dark Emerald Green

Two Candles

82 stitches by 55 stitches

DMC #	
304	Medium Christmas Red
666	Bright Christmas Red
740	Tangerine
741	Medium Tangerine
742	Light Tangerine
743	Dark Yellow
815	Medium Garnet Red
906	Medium Parrot Green
976	Medium Golden Brown
995	Dark Electric Blue
996	Medium Electric Blue

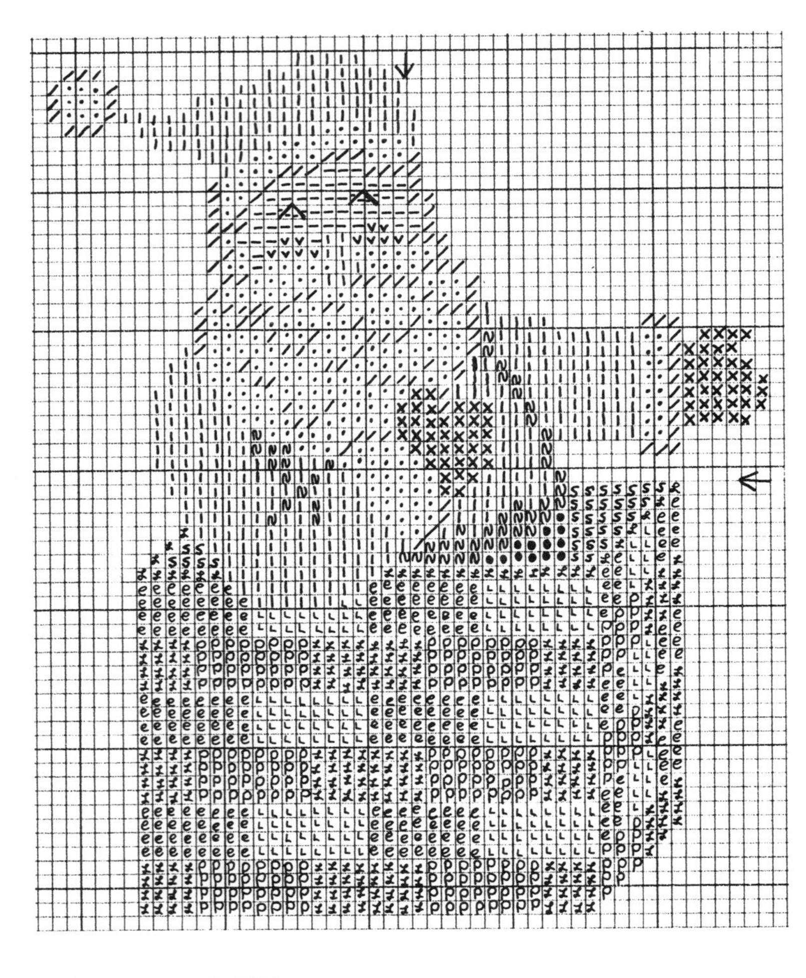

Santa and Chimney ▲

50 stitches by 62 stitches

BACK-STITCH	CROSS-STITCH	DMC #	
	S	301	Medium Mahogany
—	●	310	Black
	⊟	353	Peach
	L	402	Very Light Mahogany
	P	436	Tan
	N	498	Dark Christmas Red
	V	603	Cranberry
	I	606	Bright Orange Red
	e	780	Very Dark Topaz
	✗	801	Dark Coffee Brown
	/	828	Very Pale Blue
	X	913	Medium Nile Green
	·		White

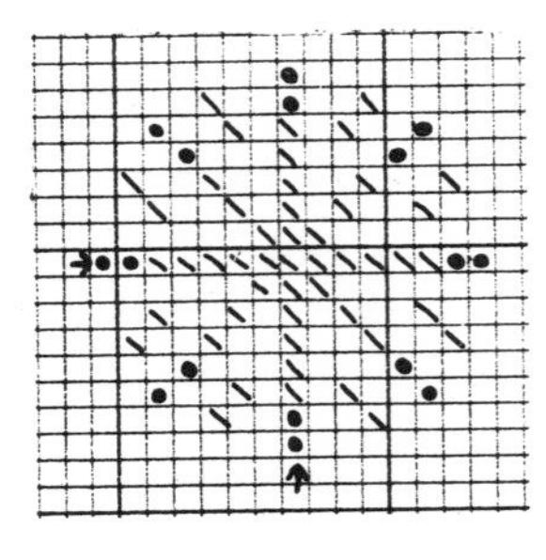

◂ *Snowflake*

15 stitches by 15 stitches

	DMC #	
●	519	Sky Blue
/	747	Very Light Sky Blue

Elf ▼

33 stitches by 66 stitches

BACK-STITCH	CROSS-STITCH	DMC #	
	●	310	Black
	V	352	Light Coral
	o	444	Dark Lemon Yellow
	I	666	Bright Christmas Red
	N	699	Christmas Green
	◣	701	Light Christmas Green
	S	702	Kelly Green
	/	704	Bright Chartreuse
~~	⊟	754	Light Peach
	e	816	Garnet Red
	L	828	Very Pale Blue
	X	995	Dark Electric Blue
	·		White

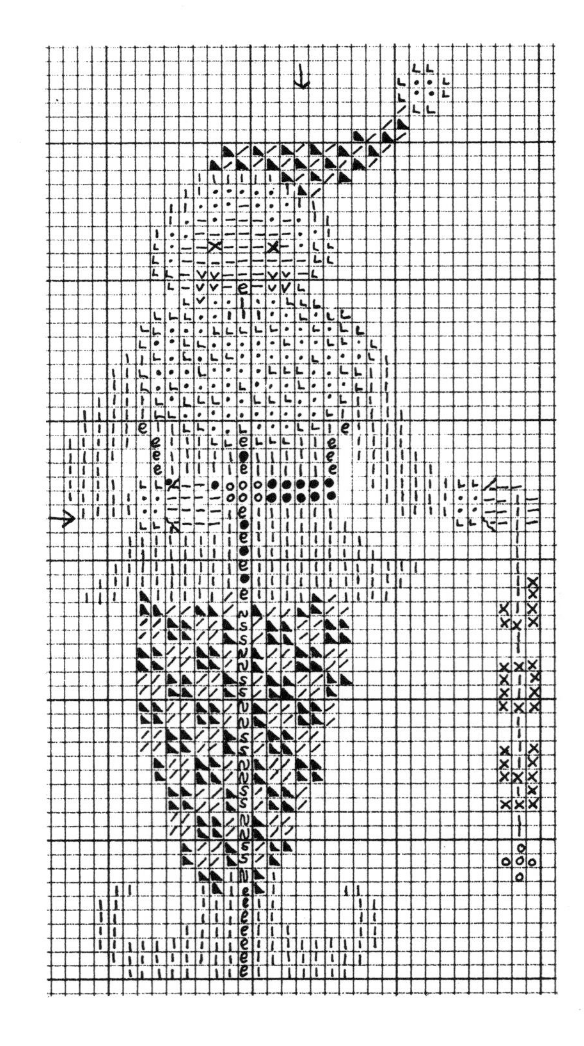

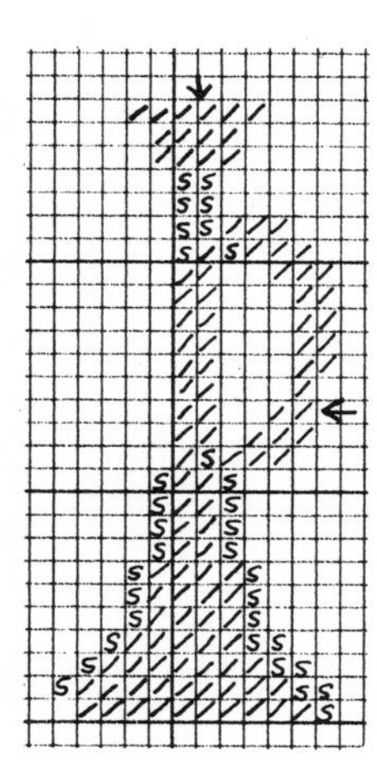

Horn

12 stitches by 27 stitches

	DMC #	
◪	725	Topaz
S	783	Christmas Gold

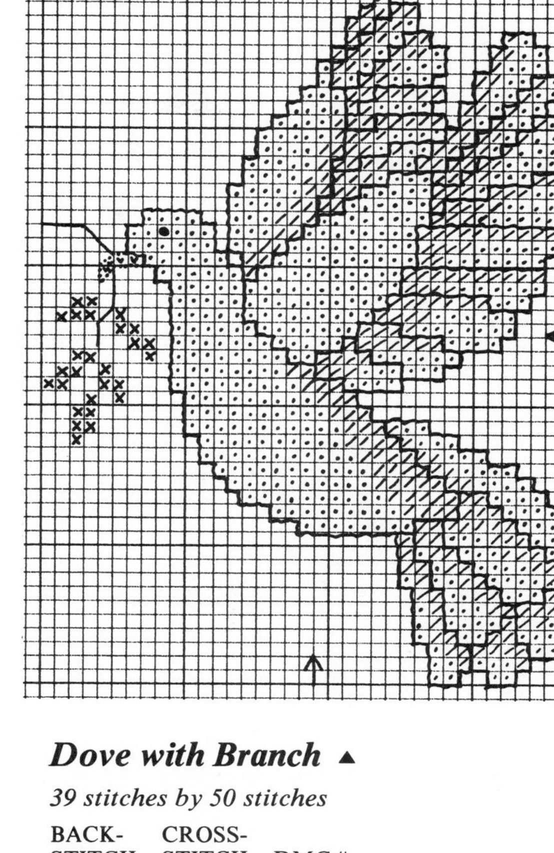

Dove with Branch

39 stitches by 50 stitches

BACK-STITCH	CROSS-STITCH	DMC #	
∿∿∿	●	341	Light Lilac
· · · ·	V	722	Medium Bittersweet
——	☒	906	Medium Parrot Green
	◪	928	Light Gray Blue
	·		White

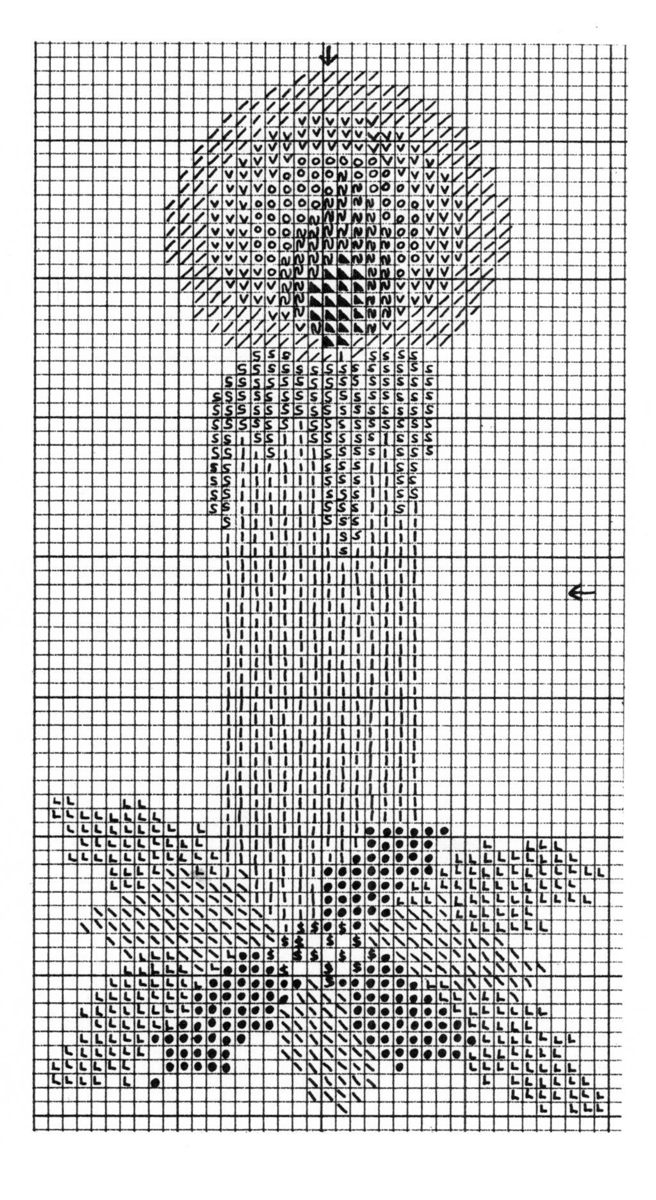

Candle

39 stitches by 75 stitches

	DMC #	
●	562	Sea Foam Green
$	606	Bright Orange Red
S	666	Bright Christmas Red
◺	704	Bright Chartreuse
◪	741	Medium Tangerine
V	742	Light Tangerine
O	743	Dark Yellow
I	816	Garnet Red
L	912	Light Emerald Green
◣	946	Medium Burnt Orange
N	947	Burnt Orange

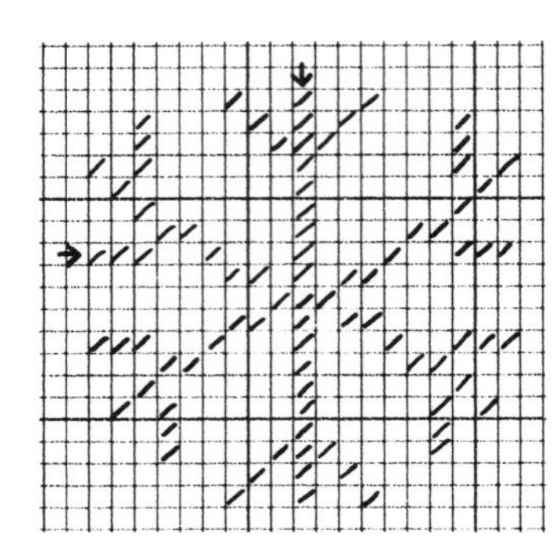

◂ Snowflake

19 stitches by 19 stitches

	DMC #	
	519	Sky Blue

Heart Stocking ▸

24 stitches by 35 stitches

BACK-STITCH	CROSS-STITCH	DMC #	
~~		666	Bright Christmas Red
		725*	Topaz
			White

*If desired, replace 725 Topaz with Balger #8 braid, Gold #002.

Tiny Candle Border ▸

9-stitch repeat by 12 stitches

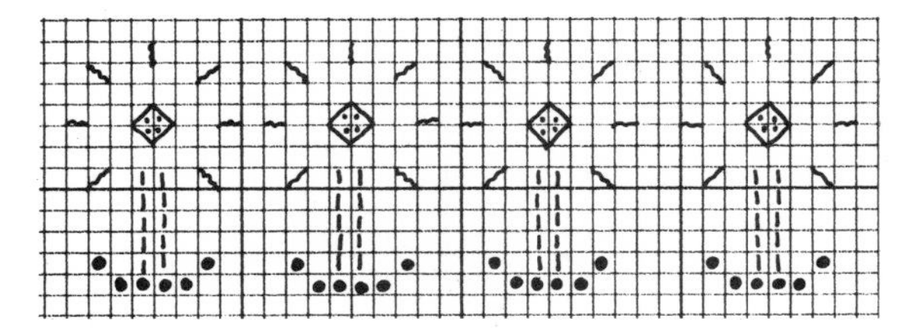

BACK-STITCH	CROSS-STITCH	DMC #	
		606	Bright Orange Red
~~		740	Tangerine
——		742	Light Tangerine
		911	Medium Emerald Green

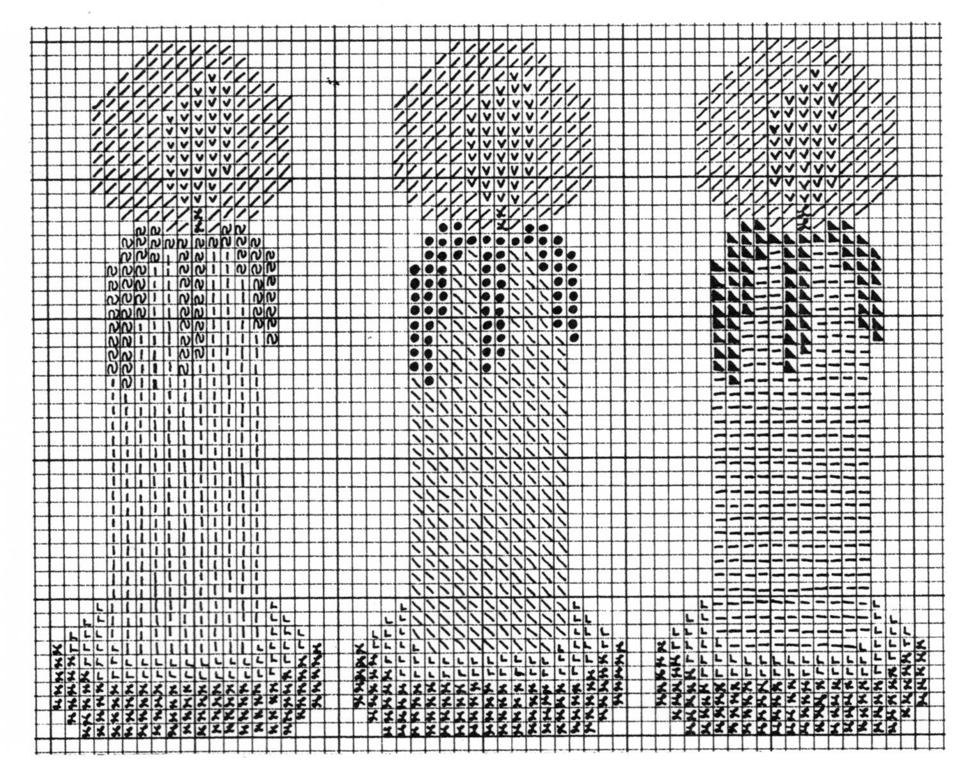

◂ Large Candle Border

21-stitch repeat by 50 stitches

	DMC #	
	433	Medium Brown
	608	Bright Orange
	666	Bright Christmas Red
	701	Light Christmas Green
	704	Bright Chartreuse
	738	Very Light Tan
	743	Dark Yellow
	947	Burnt Orange
	995	Dark Electric Blue
	996	Medium Electric Blue

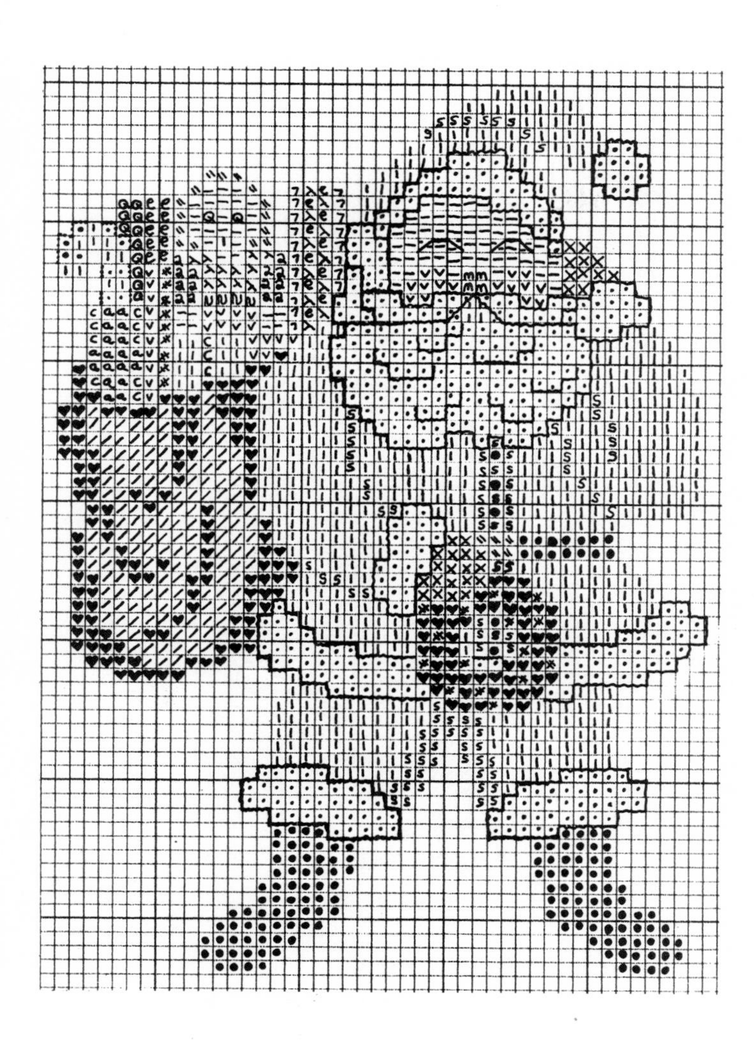

◂ *Santa with His Toy Bag*

45 stitches by 64 stitches

BACK-STITCH	CROSS-STITCH	DMC #	
		310	Black
		318	Light Steel Gray
		353	Peach
		444	Dark Lemon Yellow
		471	Light Avocado Green
		498	Dark Christmas Red
		553	Medium Violet
		603	Cranberry
		604	Light Cranberry
...		606	Bright Orange Red
		608	Bright Orange
		699	Christmas Green
		702	Kelly Green
		740	Tangerine
		742	Light Tangerine
		827	Very Light Blue
		894	Very Light Carnation
		913	Medium Nile Green
		993	Light Aquamarine
		996	Medium Electric Blue
			White

Wreath ▸

28 stitches by 33 stitches

	DMC #	
	666	Bright Christmas Red
	701	Light Christmas Green

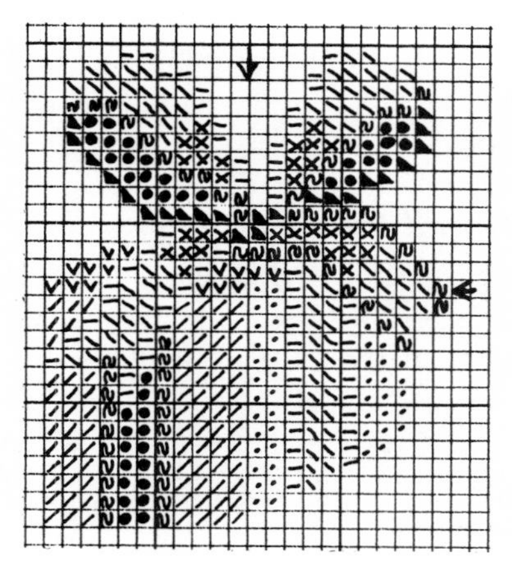

◂ *Gift Box*

22 stitches by 27 stitches

	DMC #	
	318	Light Steel Gray
	415	Pearl Gray
	606	Bright Orange Red
	666	Bright Christmas Red
	700	Bright Christmas Green
	702	Kelly Green
	704	Bright Chartreuse
	816	Garnet Red
		White

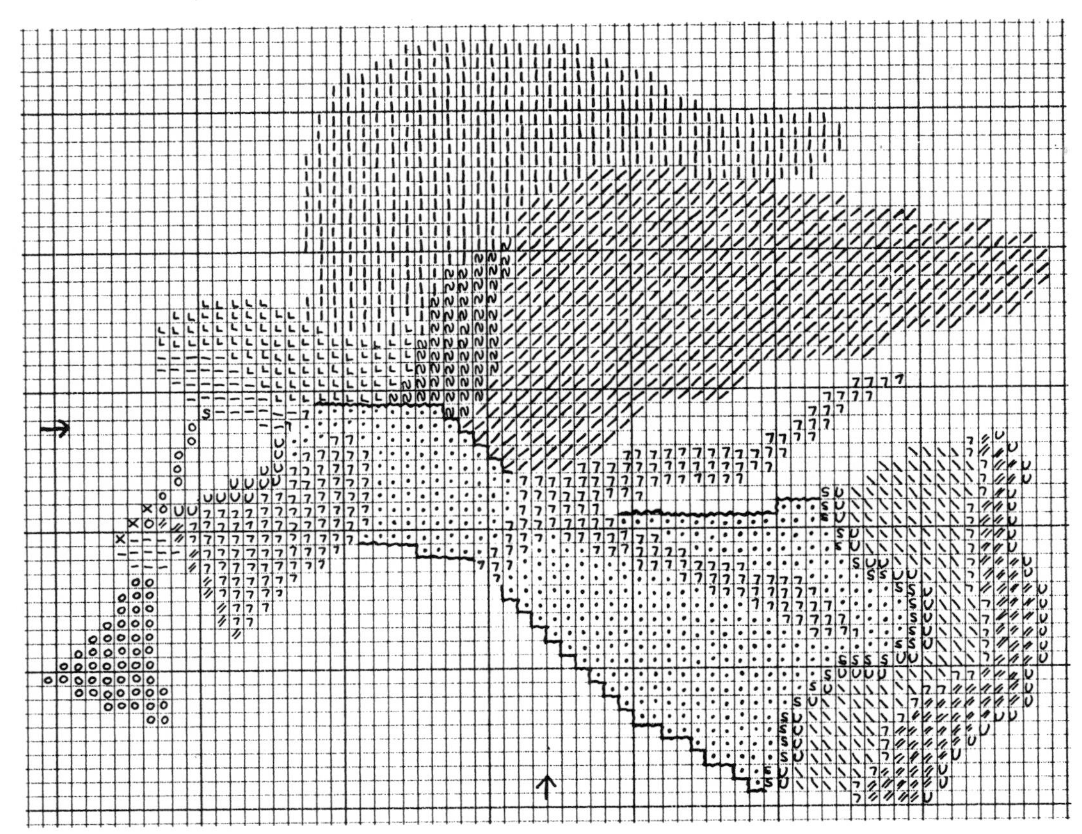

Angel ▲

71 stitches by 55 stitches

BACK-STITCH	CROSS-STITCH	DMC #	
	S	351	Coral
	X	353	Peach
	\	472	Very Light Avocado Green
	L	743	Dark Yellow
~~	7	747	Very Light Sky Blue
	–	754	Light Peach
	N	776	Medium Pink
	O	783*	Christmas Gold
	U	800	Pale Delft Blue
	//	809	Delft Blue
	I	899	Medium Rose
	/	3326	Light Rose
	•		White

*If desired, replace 783 Christmas Gold with Balger #8 braid, Gold #002.

Joyous Noel Wreath ▲

28 stitches by 28 stitches

	DMC #	
–	666	Bright Christmas Red
●	699	Christmas Green
V	702	Kelly Green
/	704	Bright Chartreuse
O	725*	Topaz
I	740	Tangerine

*If desired, replace 725 Topaz with Balger #8 braid, Gold #002.

Small Package ▸

13 stitches by 16 stitches

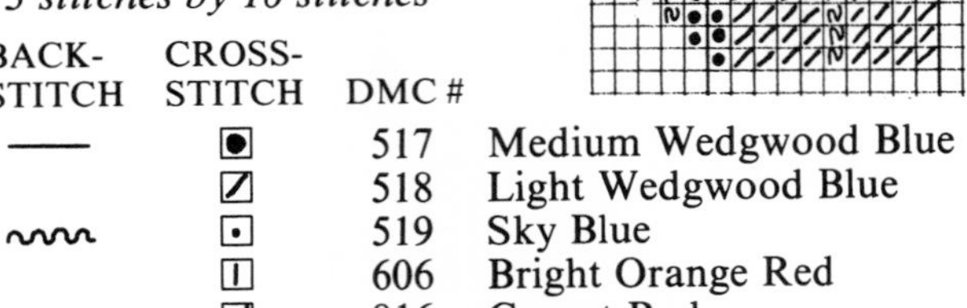

BACK-STITCH	CROSS-STITCH	DMC #	
——	●	517	Medium Wedgwood Blue
	/	518	Light Wedgwood Blue
~~	•	519	Sky Blue
	I	606	Bright Orange Red
	N	816	Garnet Red

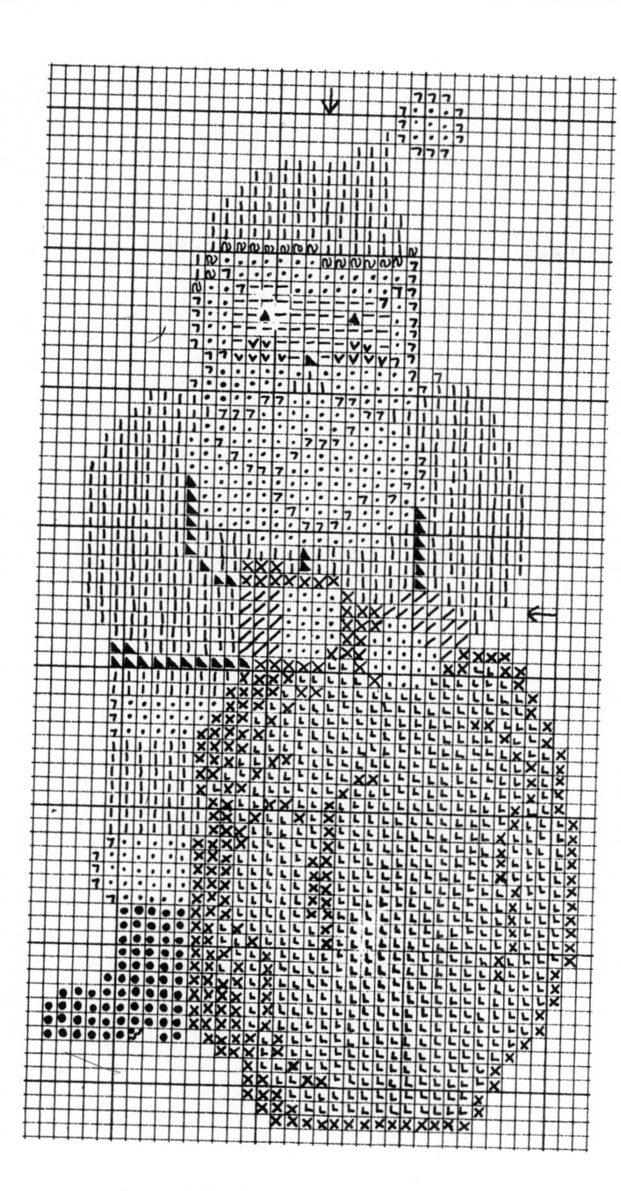

◂ *Santa and His Toy Bag*

37 stitches by 75 stitches

BACK-STITCH	CROSS-STITCH	DMC #	
∿∿∿	●	310	Black
	━	353	Peach
	▲	517	Medium Wedgwood Blue
	I	666	Bright Christmas Red
	X	699	Christmas Green
	∾	700	Bright Christmas Green
	/	701	Light Christmas Green
	L	702	Kelly Green
	◣	816	Garnet Red
	7	828	Very Pale Blue
	V	894	Very Light Carnation
	•		White

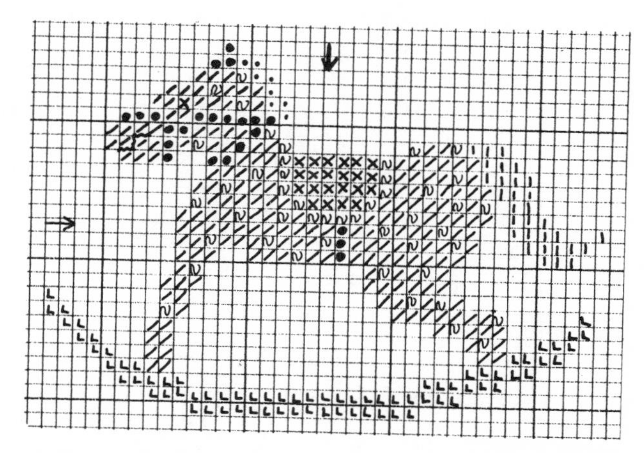

Ornament ▾

25 stitches by 28 stitches

	DMC #	
━	606	Bright Orange Red
/	704	Bright Chartreuse
●	815	Medium Garnet Red
I	996	Medium Electric Blue

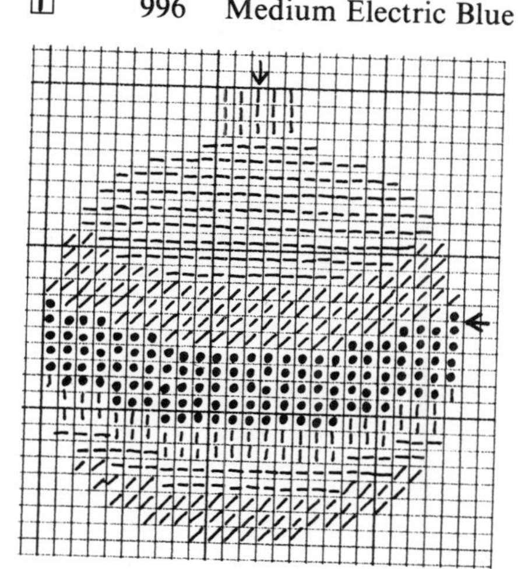

Rocking Horse ▴

39 stitches by 27 stitches

BACK-STITCH	CROSS-STITCH	DMC #	
	∾	666	Bright Christmas Red
∿∿∿	●	700	Bright Christmas Green
	/	704	Bright Chartreuse
	•	827	Very Light Blue
	L	976	Medium Golden Brown
	X	996	Medium Electric Blue
	I	3608	Fuchsia

Snowflake ▸

11 stitches by 11 stitches

	DMC #	
●	798	Dark Delft Blue
/	800	Pale Delft Blue

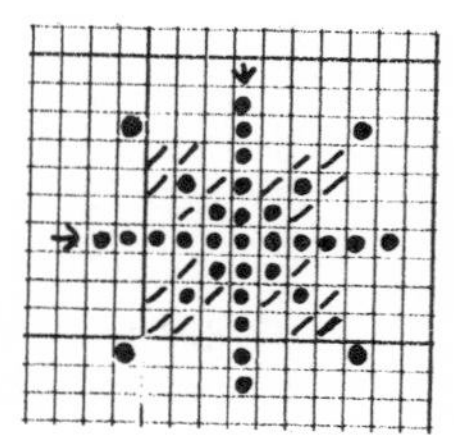

Tree ▸

32 stitches by 39 stitches

	DMC #	
☒	400	Dark Mahogany
●	517	Medium Wedgwood Blue
S	606	Bright Orange Red
V	740	Tangerine
O	743	Dark Yellow
◣	910	Dark Emerald Green
⁄	913	Medium Nile Green

Crystal Snowflake Border ▾

25-stitch repeat by 25 stitches

BACK-STITCH	CROSS-STITCH	DMC #	
	⁄	444	Dark Lemon Yellow
	L	597	Turquoise
	I	598	Light Turquoise
	N	606	Bright Orange Red
∿∿∿	◣	608	Bright Orange
	O	725*	Topaz
	⊟	740	Tangerine
	△	927*	Medium Gray Blue
—•—•—	●	995	Dark Electric Blue
	V	996	Medium Electric Blue

*If desired, replace 725 Topaz with Balger #8 braid, Gold #002 and 927 Medium Gray Blue with Balger #8 braid, Silver #001.

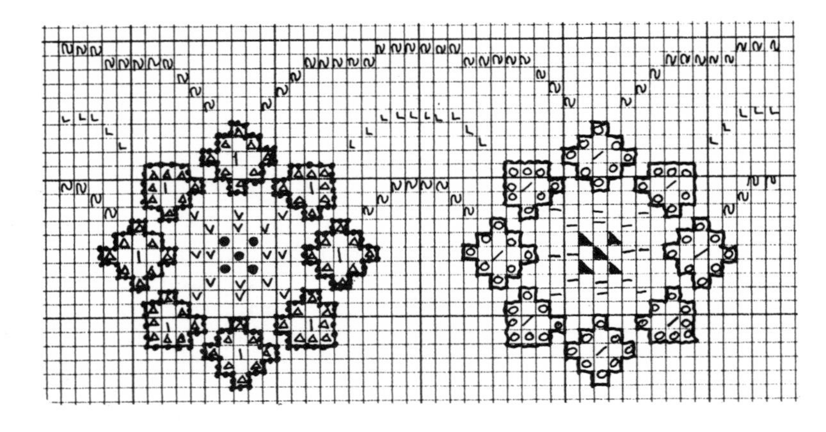

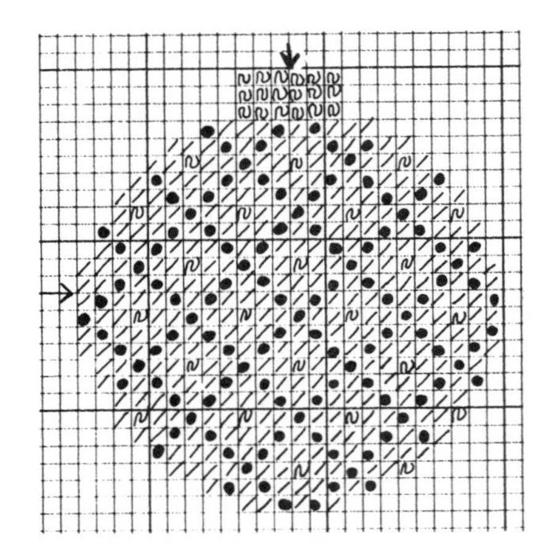

Ornament ▴

24 stitches by 26 stitches

	DMC #	
N	666	Bright Christmas Red
⁄	704	Bright Chartreuse
●	911	Medium Emerald Green

Gift Box ▸

24 stitches by 24 stitches

	DMC #	
⁄	606	Bright Orange Red
N	666	Bright Christmas Red
●	701	Light Christmas Green
L	703	Chartreuse
V	704	Bright Chartreuse
☒	741	Medium Tangerine
⊟	742	Light Tangerine
I	743	Dark Yellow
S	816	Garnet Red

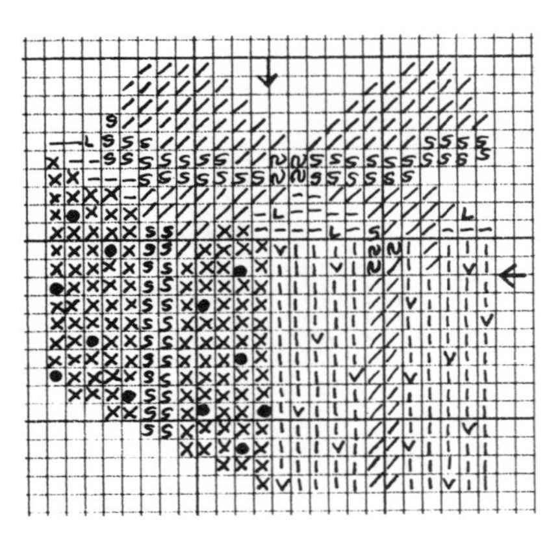

Holly Border

6 stitches by 15-stitch repeat

DMC #	
666	Bright Christmas Red
3346	Hunter Green

Gold Lantern

22 stitches by 39 stitches

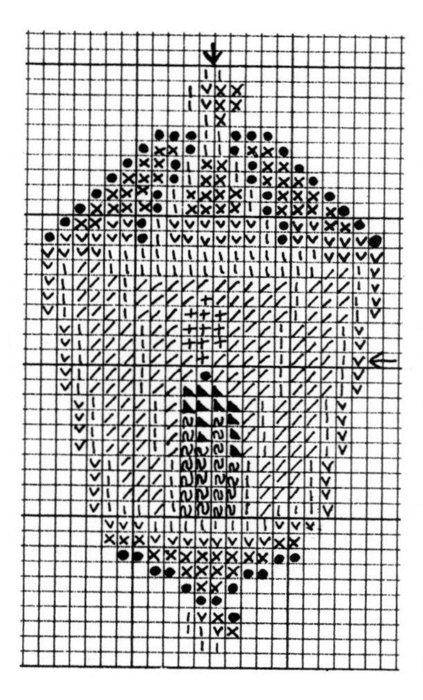

DMC #	
606	Bright Orange Red
608	Bright Orange
725	Topaz
741	Medium Tangerine
743	Dark Yellow
780	Very Dark Topaz
783	Christmas Gold
801	Dark Coffee Brown

Caroler

23 stitches by 50 stitches

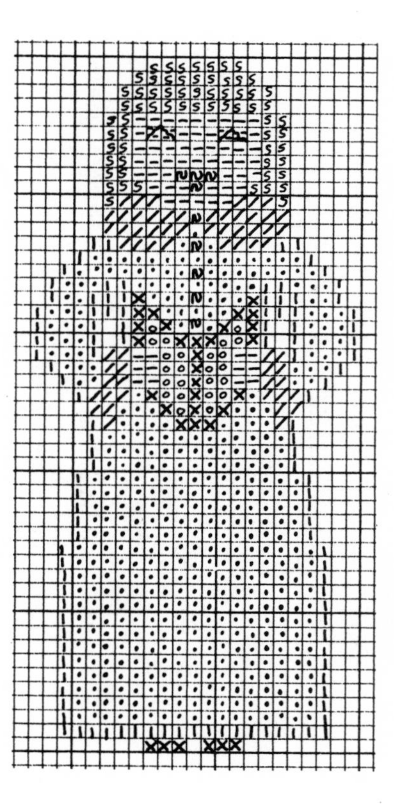

BACK-STITCH	CROSS-STITCH	DMC #	
		301	Medium Mahogany
		349	Dark Coral
		471	Light Avocado Green
		754	Light Peach
∿∿∿∿		826	Medium Blue
		977	Light Golden Brown
		3023	Light Brown Gray
			White

Noel Ornaments

60 stitches by 18 stitches

DMC #	
606	Bright Orange Red
666	Bright Christmas Red
702	Kelly Green
704	Bright Chartreuse
743	Dark Yellow
799	Medium Delft Blue
809	Delft Blue
910	Dark Emerald Green
912	Light Emerald Green

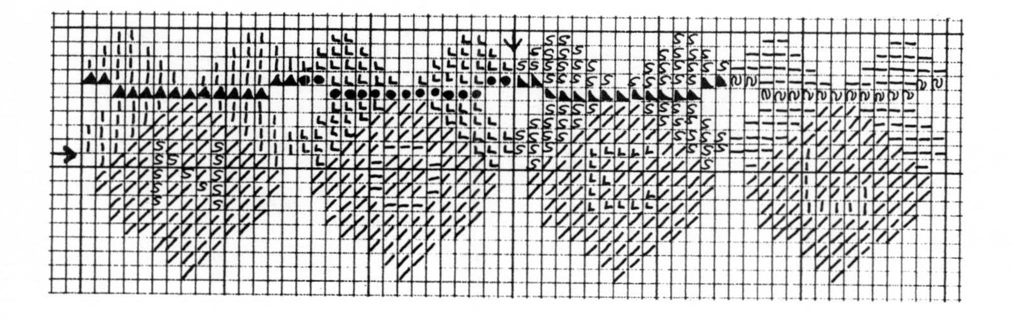

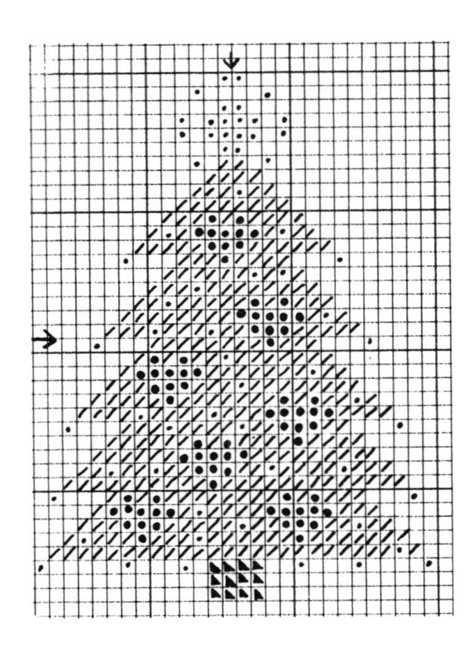

◂ *Tree and Hearts*

28 stitches by 38 stitches

	DMC #	
◙	606	Bright Orange Red
⊡	742	Light Tangerine
◣	839	Dark Beige Brown
⧄	911	Medium Emerald Green

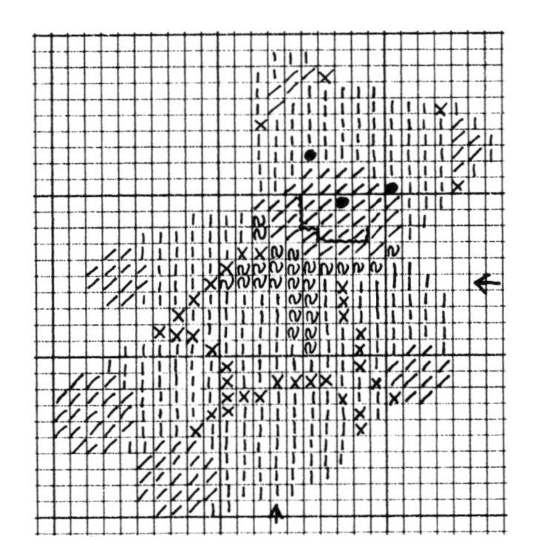

Teddy ▴

27 stitches by 29 stitches

BACK-STITCH	CROSS-STITCH	DMC #	
∿∿∿			
	◙	310	Black
	◫	435	Very Light Brown
	⧄	437	Light Tan
	∾	606	Bright Orange Red
	☒	801	Dark Coffee Brown

Ornament ▾

24 stitches by 26 stitches

	DMC #	
◫	562	Sea Foam Green
∾	666	Bright Christmas Red
⧄	742	Light Tangerine
◙	995	Dark Electric Blue

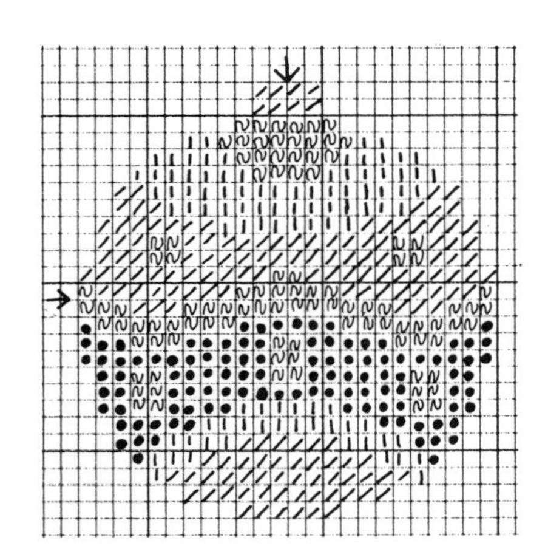

Christmas Wreath ▸

44 stitches by 46 stitches

	DMC #	
P	444	Dark Lemon Yellow
✗	519	Sky Blue
◐	603	Cranberry
○	606	Bright Orange Red
⊟	608	Bright Orange
∾	666	Bright Christmas Red
⊞	704	Bright Chartreuse
⫽	725	Topaz
V	741	Medium Tangerine
◙	815	Medium Garnet Red
⧄	910	Dark Emerald Green
♥	993	Light Aquamarine
◣	996	Medium Electric Blue
⊡		White

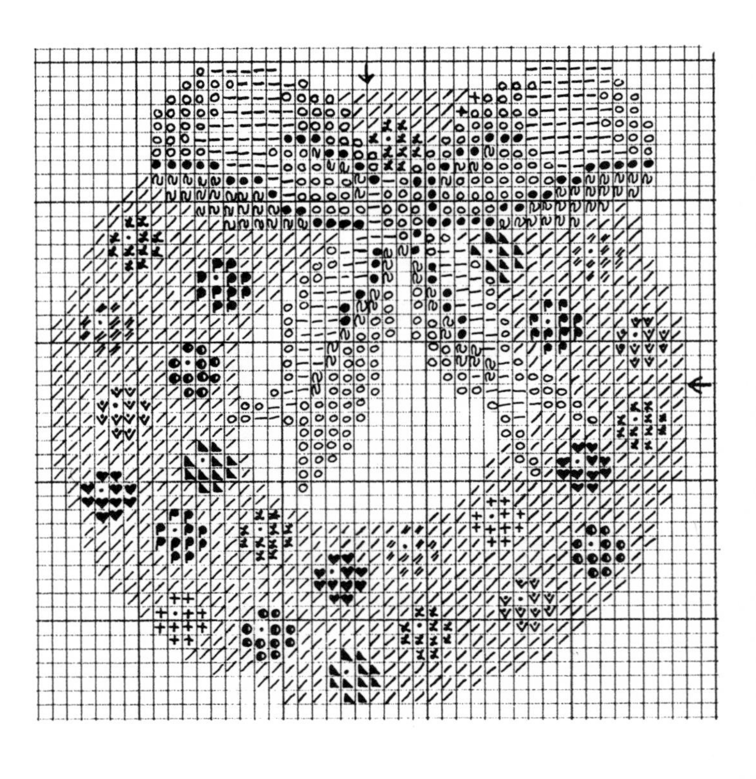

Twelve Days of Christmas ▲

70 stitches by 53 stitches

FRENCH KNOT	BACK-STITCH	CROSS-STITCH	DMC #	
	∿∿∿	●	310	Black
	- - - -	■	321	Christmas Red
		◪	415	Pearl Gray
	—•—•—	◐	433	Medium Brown
		K	435	Very Light Brown
		ℓ	437	Light Tan
		C	471	Light Avocado Green
		X	603	Cranberry
		P	646	Dark Beaver Gray
		U	647	Medium Beaver Gray
		T	648	Light Beaver Gray
	●—●—●	N	666	Bright Christmas Red
		Δ	676	Light Old Gold
		R	680	Dark Old Gold
		I	702	Kelly Green
		/	704	Bright Chartreuse
	ʌʌʌʌ	q	721	Bittersweet
	x x x	II	725	Topaz
	⊓⊔⊓	S	741	Medium Tangerine
		%	742	Light Tangerine
		O	743	Dark Yellow
		—	754	Light Peach
		K	782	Medium Topaz
		Λ	783	Christmas Gold
		t	806	Dark Peacock Blue
		B	816	Garnet Red
	• • •	◣	828	Very Pale Blue
	——	♥	910	Dark Emerald Green
		E	922	Light Copper
		H	926	Dark Gray Blue
		>	927	Medium Gray Blue
	—o—o	e	959	Aqua
•	ıııııı	◣	975	Dark Golden Brown
		♡	976	Medium Golden Brown
		//	977	Light Golden Brown
□	ooooo	✓	995	Dark Electric Blue
	—ı—ı—	♡	996	Medium Electric Blue
		3	3078	Very Light Golden Yellow
		9	3341	Light Lilac
		·		White

70 stitches by 53 stitches

See color key on page 41.

70 stitches by 53 stitches

70 stitches by 54 stitches

See color key on page 41.

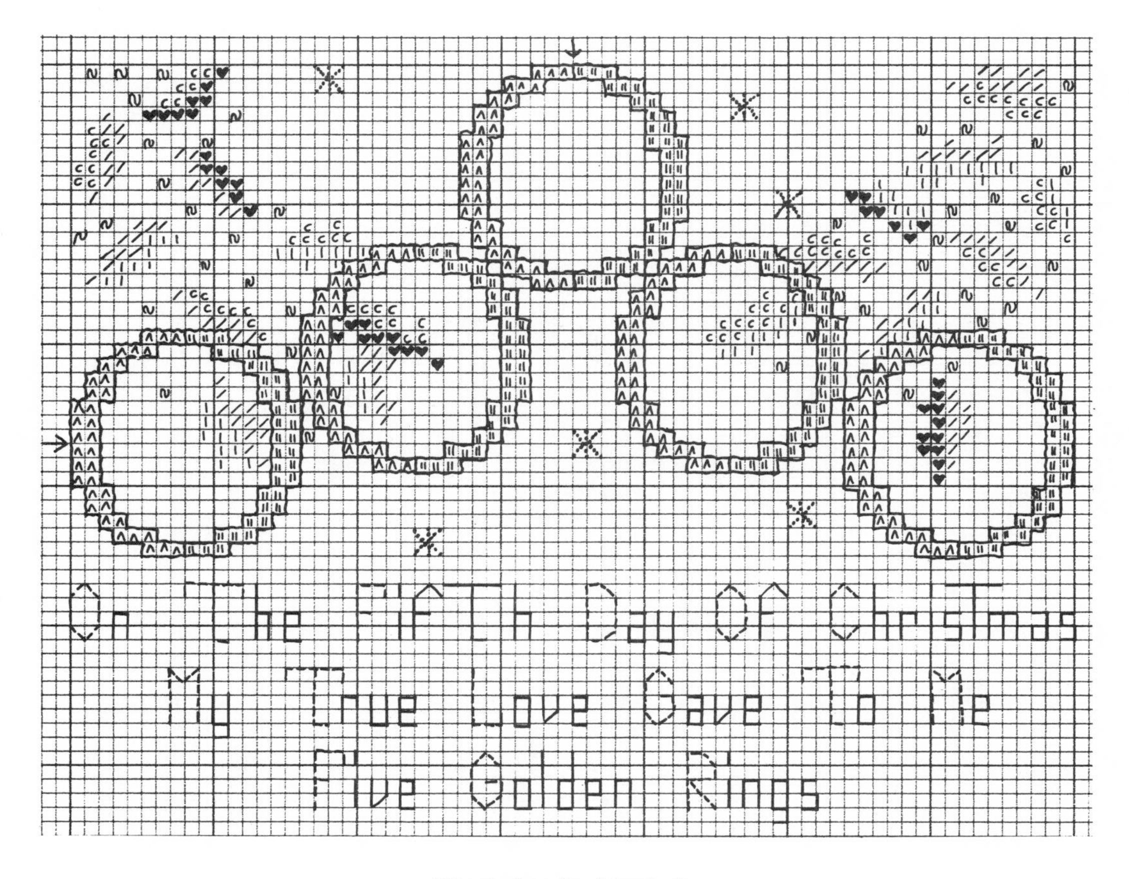

70 stitches by 54 stitches

70 stitches by 54 stitches

See color key on page 41.

70 stitches by 54 stitches

70 stitches by 53 stitches

See color key on page 41.

70 stitches by 54 stitches

70 stitches by 54 stitches

See color key on page 41.

70 stitches by 54 stitches

70 stitches by 54 stitches

See color key on page 41.

Three Trees ▸

39 stitches by 28 stitches

	DMC #	
●	801	Dark Coffee Brown
⁄	910	Dark Emerald Green

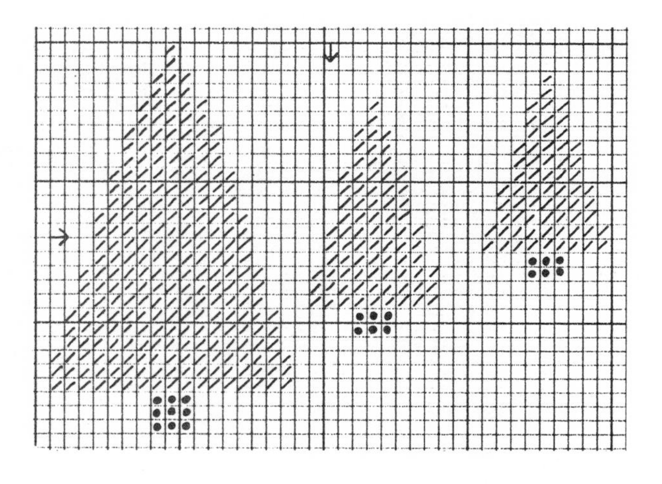

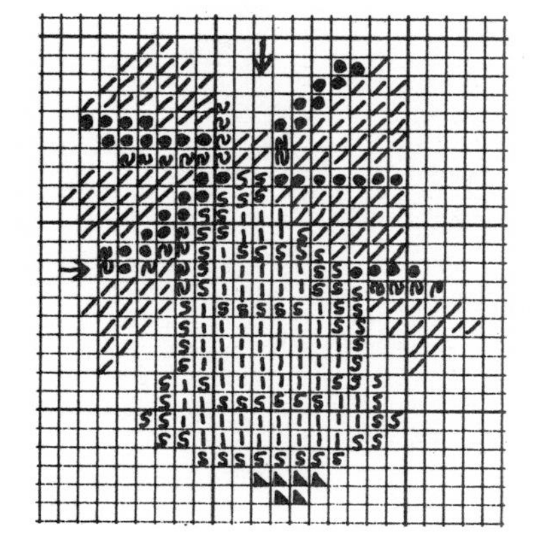

◂ *Bell*

21 stitches by 25 stitches

	DMC #	
I	606	Bright Orange Red
S	666	Bright Christmas Red
●	700	Bright Christmas Green
N	702	Kelly Green
⁄	703	Chartreuse
◣	816	Garnet Red

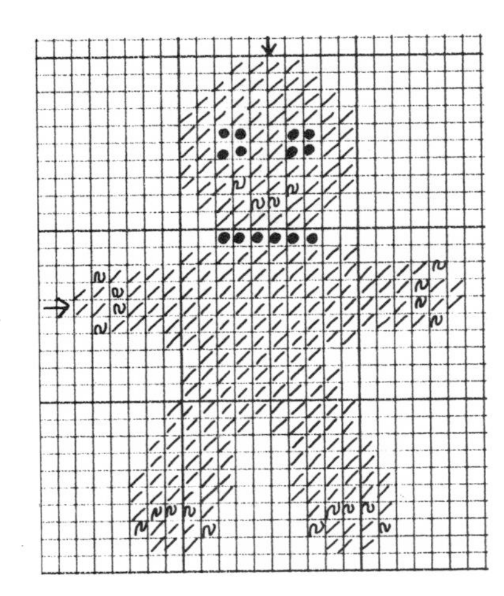

Gingerbread Man

22 stitches by 29 stitches

	DMC #	
N	666	Bright Christmas Red
/	781	Dark Topaz
•	910	Dark Emerald Green

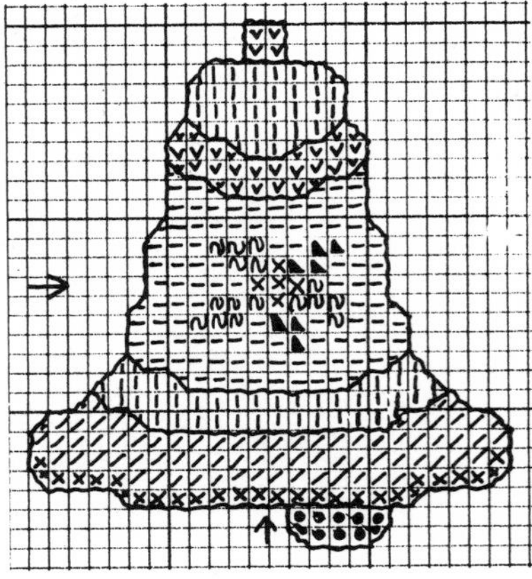

Gold Bell

24 stitches by 27 stitches

BACK-STITCH	CROSS-STITCH	DMC #	
~~	•	312	Light Navy Blue
	X	434	Light Brown
	/	444	Dark Lemon Yellow
	◣	498	Dark Christmas Red
	V	553	Medium Violet
	N	666	Bright Christmas Red
	–	910	Dark Emerald Green
	I	996	Medium Electric Blue

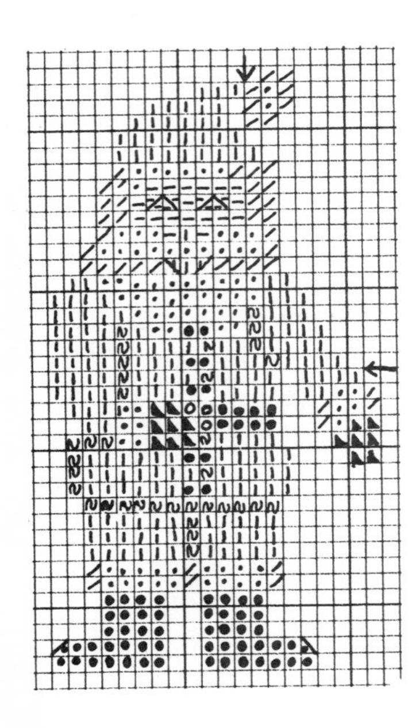

Santa

20 stitches by 38 stitches

BACK-STITCH	CROSS-STITCH	DMC #	
——	•	310	Black
	–	353	Peach
	O	444	Dark Lemon Yellow
~~	I	666	Bright Christmas Red
	/	800	Pale Delft Blue
	N	815	Medium Garnet Red
	◣	911	Medium Emerald Green
	·		White

Snowman and Heart

31 stitches by 28 stitches

BACK-STITCH	CROSS-STITCH	DMC #	
~~	◣	310	Black
	I	666	Bright Christmas Red
	S	725	Topaz
	⁒	747	Very Light Sky Blue
	X	910	Dark Emerald Green
	L	913	Medium Nile Green
	O	995	Dark Electric Blue
	/	996	Medium Electric Blue
	·		White

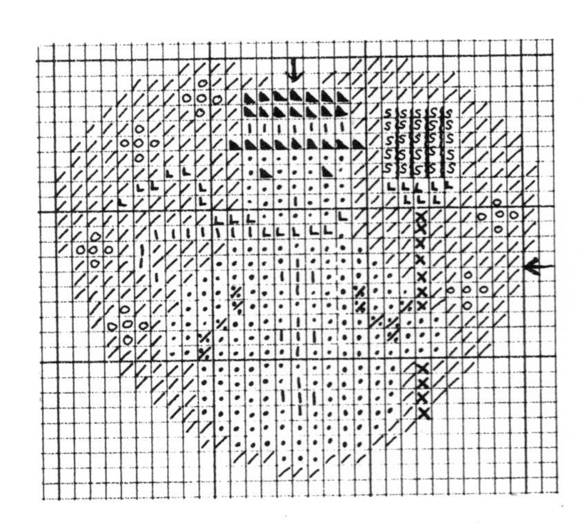